Q: HOW DO I FIND THE RIGHT JOB?

A: ASK THE EXPERTS

Q: HOW DO I FIND THE RIGHT JOB?
A: ASK THE EXPERTS

David Bowman and Ronald Kweskin

Cartoon Drawings by Howard R. Cohen

John Wiley & Sons, Inc.

New York · Chichester · Brisbane · Toronto · Singapore

ISBN 0-471-51038-6
ISBN 0-471-51039-4 (pbk.)

Printed in the United States of America

90 91   10 9 8 7 6 5 4 3 2 1

PREFACE

This book is designed to show you how to identify—and win—the *right* job. Not just *any* job, but one that will support your financial, emotional, and career needs.

We demonstrate how a thoughtful approach to job search or career change can produce a lifetime of dividends. The corporate job market is changing rapidly. The decade ahead will see further radical change. Awareness, understanding, and appreciation of these issues is your best safeguard against being counted among the tens of thousands of employees who are currently dissatisfied and unhappy in their jobs, or will be facing career changes in the years ahead.

ACKNOWLEDGMENTS

We wish to extend our grateful appreciation to Maggie Doud, Kimberle Baxter, and Katherine Lavalle for their invaluable assistance during the preparation of this book. Our special appreciation must also be extended to Dick Rinella who so generously shared with us his considerable knowledge and expertise.

CONTENTS

Can I objectively assess myself? 12 What can I learn about myself
that I don't already know? 13 I know myself pretty well. Is all
this assessment necessary? 14 But not everyone has the luxury of
passing up job offers until the right one comes along,
right? 14 What else can I learn from self-assessment? 15 Okay,
how do I begin self-assessment? 15 Identify my accomplishments? That shouldn't take long. 21 How can past accomplishments help me now? 22 What exactly do you consider an
accomplishment? 22 How far back should I go? 23 Now that
I've completed my assessment exercises—whew!—how do I use
them? 28 Threading? What's that? 28 Don't I need help threading? Can I really do it myself? 29 Can you show me how threading works? 29 Once I have done my threading, what else is
left? 31 What exactly do you mean by career-goal-setting, and
how does it work? 34 How do I set career goals? 34 How can
anyone plan ten years into the future? 35 What if my goal is to
become a CEO in ten years? 35 All of this sounds very calculat-
ing. Shouldn't life be more spontaneous? 36 How can I figure out
my long- and short-term goals? 36 Once I have established my
goals, how often should I review them? 40 In addition to assess-
ing myself, should I consider outside vocational testing? 41 What
about career counselors? Should I see one? 41 What about
changing industries? How can I do that in the nineties? 42

Contents

help? 86 How do search firms get paid? 86 How do I locate and get in touch with an executive search firm? 87 Are search firms really worth the bother? 88 If a search firm calls me, how should I respond? What do I tell them? 88 Once I have been called by a search firm, how soon will I know if I am a candidate for a job? 89 If I send my resume to one office of a national search firm or employment agency, will it be on their computer for other offices? 90 What about employment agencies? Should I consider them? 90 Are there any other published sources for jobs? 90

Contents

INTRODUCTION

The history of humankind is liberally sprinkled with jobs that used to be. When word of mouth was replaced by the printed word, the venerable town crier was sent packing; Edison put the lamplighter out of business; just a generation or two back, everyone knew their ice man, milk man, and coal man. The job you are doing today probably won't need doing by the year 2000, at least not in the way you're doing it now.

Driven by technology and a shift in demographic make-up, work and lifestyle changes are occurring at a dizzying pace. The information age, ushered in by the computer, the aging population, the changing business climate for women and minorities, as well as the globalization of business—these are among the many causes. The result, by some estimates, will be that eighty percent of today's occupations will disappear within the next fifteen years. Most workers will have changed jobs three to five times, careers twice, and will be in professions that have not yet evolved.[1]

By the year 2000, today's computer will have become a relic. The new generations of computers will bring about startling advances such as practical artificial intelligence, which will lead in turn to extraordinarily rapid product development and manufacturing processes. We are likely to witness a product move from concept through development into the marketplace in the space of weeks instead of months or years.

Electronic storage will make business information available to everyone in the blink of an eye. Information advisory services for non-routine information will be easily accessible through on-line networks. Electronic self-diagnostic devices will become common-place. As a matter of fact, the diagnostic computer for automobiles is already a reality; heavy machinery and your washer–dryer can't be far behind. By the year 2000, we will probably see robots designed entirely for the purpose of directing other robots![2]

America, which in the late eighteenth and early nineteenth cen-turies moved from an agricultural society to an industrial society, is now in the process of another dramatic shift. John Naisbitt, in his book *Megatrends,* sees us becoming an informational society. Others have called it a service society. According to Naisbitt, white collar workers outnumbered blue collar workers for the first time in our history in 1956; in other words, more Americans worked with infor-mation or in service areas than produced goods.

Furthermore, professional workers are now the second largest oc-cupational classification. These are nearly all *information* workers: lawyers, teachers, engineers, computer programmers, systems ana-lysts, doctors, architects, accountants, librarians, newspaper report-ers, social workers, nurses, clergy, and so on. Between 1960 and 1981, this group more than doubled in size, increasing from 7.5 mil-lion to 16.4 million, and nearly one-half were women![3] That trend has continued through the eighties and will continue through the nineties and into the next century.

If you are a manufacturing worker, the prognosis is anything but good. The World Future Society predicts that manufacturing workers in the United States will drop from twenty-eight percent of the total work force in 1980 to three percent by the year 2030.[4] And a joint study from the U.S. Department of Labor and Digital Equipment Cor-poration predicts that by the year 2000, manufacturing employment will decline by more than 800,000 jobs.[5]

Naisbitt, as well as many other futurists, don't predict the disap-pearance of the manufacturing/industrial sector of American business, but, rather, its transference to Third-World countries where labor is plentiful and far less expensive.

So, American society is shifting from an industrial focus to one of information and service, and a major contributing factor is the relatively high cost of American labor. But are there other less obvious currents running through American society that may well be as significant as the cost of labor, factors that inevitably will have a profound effect on future employment and your choice of a career? You bet! Demographics, for example.

Our current obsession with youth notwithstanding, we are in the midst of what some have dubbed "the graying of America." Like it or not, America is getting *older*. We are also not reproducing: in other words, we're facing a "birth dearth."

According to U.S. Census Bureau predictions, by the year 2000 the number of Americans between the ages of twenty-five and thirty-four will drop by 8.2 percent, or 2.2 million people. Simultaneously, and with breathtaking acceleration, the number of Americans between the ages of forty-five and fifty-four will increase by a whopping fifty-four percent, or 13.1 million, representing the leading edge of the baby boomers.[6]

The Census Bureau also projects that by the turn of the century, there will be more than 35 million Americans over the age of sixty-five. Less conservative predictions are that by the year 2000—with continued improvements in lifestyle and medical technology—we are likely to see some 40 to 45 million Americans over age sixty-five. That's approximately one-fifth of the total population.[7] The Rand Corporation, a California think tank, projects that by the year 2000 the average life expectancy *at birth* will be over ninety years, this due to continued improvements in health care, disease prevention, pharmacology, genetic engineering, bionics, and organ transplantation.[8]

Currently, the over-fifty population is just about 60 million strong (nearly one-quarter of our entire population) and has a combined personal income of over $800 billion! That demographic group also controls seventy percent of the net worth of U.S. households—nearly $7 *trillion!*[9]

But let's go back to the ever-popular baby boomers. If you were born between 1946 and 1964, you qualify. You are also one of 76 million others, a full one-third of America's population.

But just so that impressive figure doesn't go to your head, consider these facts for a moment. In 1990, you will be between the ages of twenty-six and forty-four. As we celebrate the coming of the new century—only the blink of an eye away—some of you will be nearing the age of early retirement.

And, at the same time that America is graying, it has been predicted that twenty percent of you boomers will have no children; another twenty-five percent will have only one child. Coupled with the fact that the present fertility rate of American women is 1.8 (representing the projected number of children each woman will have in her lifetime), it is fair to conclude—if that rate continues—that we aren't replacing ourselves.[10]

What does all this mean? Most likely, it means that the coming "senior boom" and "birth dearth" will create a focus on the needs and desires of the middle-aged and the elderly in the population, and, due to the heightened attention given to financial planning, retirement/pension plans, etc., these individuals will be able to pay for what they want!

The impact of all these factors will reverberate throughout our economy like shock waves radiating from the epicenter of an earthquake. The Bureau of Labor Statistics points out that because the labor force is going to increasingly lose more workers to early retirement, without sufficient numbers to replace them, there will be labor shortages—creating more opportunities for minorities, immigrants, and part-time workers. Also pointed out is the growing gap between the skills needed for the new informational/service jobs and the skills currently possessed by the work force.[11] This gap will create significant opportunities in training and education. It is also expected that by the nineties, two-thirds of the new work-force entrants will be women, which should produce collateral opportunities in child care, both in and outside the home, as well as at the work place.[12]

For the most part, we have been looking inward, or domestically, to uncover evidence that can lead us to some logical assessment of the future, but unless we broaden our investigation, an incomplete picture will emerge.

In less than half a century, modern technology has created a global society. Russian teenagers wear jeans and listen to contemporary American music. American teenagers can watch their counterparts in Beijing demonstrate for reform—while it is happening. Space exploration, satellite transmission, supersonic jet aircraft—each new development has effectively reduced the size of the earth we inhabit. Cooperation among people and nations has become a prescription for survival. Like it or not, we live in a global society, with interconnected economies and mutual business interests. These commonalities will undoubtedly shape and influence many of our career choices for decades to come.

The globalization of business has already begun. For example, in *Megatrends,* John Naisbitt describes the "world car"—an automobile assembled in one country, from parts manufactured in another country (or countries), produced as a joint-venture partnership between companies from still other countries.

GM and Toyota produce an automobile together at a plant in California. Honda, Nissan, and Volkswagen have all made vehicles in America. Volkswagen produces parts in Mexico and Brazil; Mitsubishi has provided engines for various Chrysler cars; Ford's Escort is assembled in several countries from parts manufactured and imported from other countries.[13]

The automotive business is, of course, only one of many that have already become globalized. There are major international companies such as our own General Electric, Japan's Hitachi, and Germany's Siemens that are virtually world trading companies. They compete with one another all over the globe and frequently barter something they make for something made in another country, which they then sell elsewhere to realize a profit. This type of mega-company bartering frequently occurs with countries in the Eastern bloc, Africa, and Asia, where hard currency is exactly that, hard to come by.[14]

Then consider the globalization of energy, fashion and textiles, entertainment, medicine and medical equipment, aerospace, food and beverages, information processing, electronics, and banking to name only a few. These are all *world* industries, not just American, with interconnecting countries and companies providing worldwide financing, manufacturing, and distribution.

Clearly, the marketplace for jobs during the next decade and beyond will be marked by profound change. Further advances in technology, the graying of America, corporate restructuring and globalization, as well as changing market demands will result in the creation of new jobs and new career paths. But economics and business, like physics, follows each action with a reaction. The forces that usher in new opportunity are likely to do so at the expense of older job functions and perhaps even entire occupations.

In the pages that follow, we will try to awaken in you an appreciation of the changing landscape of American business and its probable effect on the future job market. Our emphasis will remain on searching for jobs and planning careers. Without a thorough understanding of both of these areas, success will be less likely. As competition heats up for good jobs in the decade ahead, your ability to conduct a thorough and effective job search will become more important than ever before.

Early in 1989, we conducted an extensive survey in which we asked the human resource directors at many of America's largest corporations to comment on a variety of job-search subjects. The purpose of the survey was to provide a "hiring-line" professional's perspective on the often confusing, sometimes contradictory, advice we are given when facing the not inconsiderable task of finding a new job. These men and women were generous in their comments, sharing with us their own individual standards and expectations. They reveal not only a few surprises, but a consistency of thought that must be taken seriously. Their comments are scattered throughout the pages of this book, and we hope you find them helpful in understanding and implementing the job-search process.

Finally, we have identified and analyzed a number of career fields that look like a good bet for the future.

No one has a crystal ball. The future will always remain clouded by distance and altered by spontaneous events. But a body of evidence usually precedes and signals the coming of significant change. Those among you who remain alert to the evidence and prepare for the transition will prosper. As John F. Kennedy once said: "Change is the law of life. And those who look only to the past or the present are certain to miss the future."

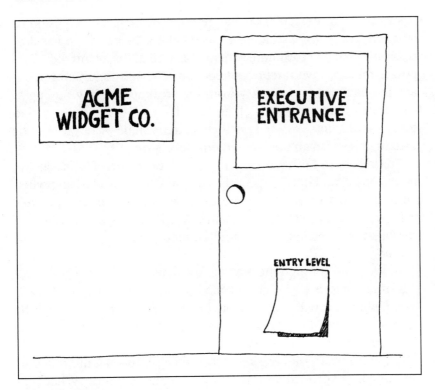

Strategies for the 90s

Loyalty

"You're on your own. Job security is a discounted commodity in an environment more individual than organizational, more opportunistic than secure. Decline of loyalty [by corporations toward their employees] cuts both ways, and working people don't put their trust in companies or unions anymore."
  • James Flanigan, columnist for the *Los Angeles Times*, 3/5/89

"Cradle-to-grave" company loyalty? Don't count on it—it's over! The corporate loyalty that once gave a worker lifetime employment simply is not there anymore, and the situation is likely to get worse before it gets better.

Government deregulation has resulted in mergers, acquisitions, and divestitures on a scale never seen before. Deregulation has dramatically changed corporate America, as well as the job market. Corporate raiders, investment bankers, lawyers, and top management are all benefiting handsomely from the breakup and re-grouping of corporate assets, but all too often the "little guy"—the workers who helped build those assets into their current value—are given their walking papers in an unceremonious downsizing.

So, the control of your career is yours. Be aware of what's going on out there, and don't expect the company to be loyal to you when outside suitors or raiders come a-calling. Loyalty in the nineties will continue to decrease as international corporate spin-offs and combinations become even more commmonplace, both here and abroad.

As we move through the nineties and beyond, one consequence of this situation is that workers will job hop much more frequently than ever before and will not be thought of badly for it. People will be more loyal toward their own careers than toward the companies for which they work. And perhaps that's the way it should be.

A client of ours who was recently displaced from a California utility company expressed his frustration with this question: "What happened? I was supposed to have a job for life!" He then went on to say that the company had even used this concept of lifetime loyalty in its recruitment of him many years before.

He was recruited a long time ago, however, and he hadn't realized that the corporate world had changed. Once on the outside, our friend soon discovered that based on his responsibilities, experience, and abilities he had been substantially underpaid. His mistake? Turning the management of his career over to someone else, namely, his employer. Although it is often better to move up than out, sometimes it is *wise* to move out in order to get a different perspective on the working world.

What changes do you foresee in the decade ahead?

"**Reduced loyalty** on the part of the employer. Increased number of mergers and acquisitions. A greater number of college grads choosing to be more independent. Jobs will become more 'contractual.'"

- Gary Bernard, Senior Vice President/Human Resources, Dataproducts Corporation

---

"Currently, employers still hold the power of selection for good candidates, particularly at the higher levels. Within the next ten years, I believe employers will be begging good managerial talent to work for them. It will be a candidates' market—they will call on companies to put forward their desires, etc. And the company offering the most flexibility—compensation, benefits, etc.—will be picked. Companies will be seeking seasoned, experienced managers, not young hot shots out of college, to manage their people, assets, and quality of services or products."

- Vera Blanchet, Vice President/Human Resources, Corporate Headquarters, California Federal Savings & Loan Association

---

Notes

1. Jeffrey J. Hallett, *Workplace Visions* (Alexandria, Va.: American Society for Personnel Administration, n.d.), as quoted in *Personal Report* (New York: March 1988).

2. "Careers Beyond the Millenium," *Personal Report* (New York: February 1989).

3. John Naisbitt, *Megatrends* (New York: Warner Books, 1982), pp. 1–9.

4. "Careers Beyond the Millenium," *Personal Report* (New York: March 1988).

5. Martha I. Finney, "Planning Today for the Future's Changing Shape," *Personnel Administration* (January 1989), pp. 44, 45.

6. Sharon Bernstein, "New Market Predictions for an Aging Population," *Los Angeles Herald Examiner* (April 24, 1989).

7. Dychtwald, Ken, and Joe Flower, *Age Wave* (Los Angeles: Tarcher, 1989), p. 8.

8. Ibid.

9. Ibid., p. 10.

10. Ibid., p. 268.

11. Ibid., p. 13.

12. Ibid., pp. 11–12.

13. Ann McLaughlin, "The Pig in the American Python," *Los Angeles Times* (April 2, 1989).

14. John Naisbitt, *Megatrends* (New York: Warner Books, 1982), pp. 65, 66.

CHAPTER ONE

WHO AM I?
WHAT AM I?
WHERE AM I GOING?

Everyone's looking for the *right* job, and why not? Only a fool would look for the *wrong* job, right? Wrong.

Now, you're probably saying: "Get serious. No one would actually look for the wrong job." To which we'd answer: "Sure they would. And do!" Perhaps not consciously, but that's a minor difference. The end result is usually the same.

Many of us don't give a great deal of thought to whether a job can support and satisfy our internal needs, and more than a few of us don't give a whole lot of thought to anything at all. But, if you are going to find the *right* job, it is not a bad idea to know what you are looking for and why.

If you are seeking a job that offers a high degree of personal satisfaction and an opportunity for career advancement, you had better look beyond such external needs as salary, fringe benefits, title, etc. Each of these factors must be carefully considered, but if the job itself is not a comfortable fit, you probably won't be around long enough to enjoy them.

What do we mean by a comfortable fit? Well, let's assume, for example, that you're the kind of person who finds it difficult to perform well under close supervision; you need a certain degree of freedom in order to be productive. If this were the case, you would be well advised to avoid companies whose method of operation is highly structured and closely supervised. No doubt you would find the fit very uncomfortable. On the other hand, if your personal needs require structure and close supervision, the fit might be perfect.

The point is, you can't define the *right* job without first having defined yourself. To ignore this fact is to invite the possibility of a dangerous error in judgment. The introspective process that encourages you to probe and discover the special qualities that are distinctly yours is called self-assessment. It is the subject of this first chapter, and a very important starting point for a successful job search.

Can I Objectively Assess Myself?

Sure you can. In fact, there's probably no one better suited for the job. We're not talking about psychoanalysis. We're talking about taking a long hard look at the job you're in, or have just left, or hope to find. How have things been going? What do you want or expect from the future? How will you achieve your goals? Do you have any goals? What are your strengths? Are you aware of your weaknesses? Are you comfortable working in a group, or do you prefer working alone? The answer to these and several other similar questions will provide you with a deeper understanding of yourself and a secure foundation for intelligent choice.

At the end of this chapter, you will find a number of exercises you can complete yourself. When doing the exercises, try to remember that they are not tests, and you are not being graded *good* or *bad*, *pass* or *fail*. They are simply exercises designed to help you define yourself, perhaps for the very first time. We have also included some suggestions for vocational and aptitude testing, which we strongly recommend you consider.

What changes do you foresee in the decade ahead?

"The 1990's will definitely be an employees' market. Well-trained job candidates (and perhaps those not so well-trained) will find employers' doors wide open. The shrinking labor force should provide fierce competition among employers seeking to fill their quotas. Among other things, this should mean high salaries for even the relative novice."

- Denny Wheeler, Manager, Corporate Human Resources, B. F. Goodrich

---

"**In retailing,** there are fewer and fewer department store organizations and they are becoming huge. These companies, primarily as a function of size, tend to be bureaucratic and less flexible in their hiring of executives. This means they normally focus on a highly defined candidate profile—similar to the IBM's or large accounting firms of an earlier era. Individuals who fall outside of the "ideal" candidate profile will probably not be hired. The very diversity that has characterized department store retailing and made it exciting will be lost.

It appears to me that specialty retailing will, therefore, represent an attractive opportunity for many. Certainly most specialty organizations will also seek "main stream" candidates, but they will continue to provide greater opportunities for the more creative, independent and entrepreneurial job seekers."

- Olon P. Zager, Director of Human Resources, Gucci

What Can I Learn About Myself That I Don't Already Know?

Possibly nothing. At least, nothing you haven't sensed at one time or another. But you may rediscover some things you had forgotten. The process of self-assessment is not specifically intended to uncover and reveal breathtaking new insights. Its purpose and value is to force you to dig deeply, to re-acquaint yourself with the characteristics that make you unique, as each of us is.

Most of us tend to wear our strengths on our sleeves and bury our weaknesses deep beneath a protective fabric. The danger here is that our weaknesses—and we all have them—are sometimes buried so deeply that they are forgotten. When we bury and forget our weaknesses, it is altogether possible to accept a job offer that actually plays to our weaknesses rather than to our strengths. Taking such a job will almost always lead to frustration and failure.

I Know Myself Pretty Well. Is All This Assessment Necessary?

You bet it is. Career advancement is not as simple as stepping onto an escalator and being carried to the top. From entry level to retirement you will be faced with important decisions, many of which will commit you to a course of action that is not easily reversed or changed. The correctness of those decisions will play a major, if not critical, role in your career advancement. Informed and thoughtful decisions are your best protection against errors of judgment. Self-knowledge is an endless game that must be played out at every stage of your life.

"**With the increased advent** of mergers and acquisitions, which in most cases end up in a consolidation of job functions, I believe that early on in one's career a specific expertise in one's given area is extremely important. Develop a skill or knowledge to the highest possible level and achieve a reputation for that ability. With that in hand, the person becomes valuable within the organization—too valuable to let go."
 • James J. Carter, Principal, Avery Crafts Associates Ltd.

But Not Everyone Has the Luxury of Passing Up Job Offers Until the Right One Comes Along, Right?

Yes, that's absolutely true. Personal circumstances may dictate your course of action, but, even so, if you know you have accepted a job that normally would not be your first choice, your sense of self-awareness is heightened. Having identified the problem areas in advance, you will be better equipped to confront them. Also, in today's business climate, no job is considered a permanent commitment. Do the best you can. If the job works out, fine, but if it doesn't, don't hesitate to look elsewhere. The worst mistake you can possibly make is to stay in the wrong job longer than necessary.

What Else Can I Learn from Self-Assessment?

Self-assessment (which also includes re-assessment) serves another important purpose as well. It provides you with an opportunity to freeze the action, to get off the treadmill just long enough to take stock of your life and career direction. This taking stock is absolutely essential because you can't take corrective action unless you have first realized that it is necessary.

Many people wander aimlessly through life only vaguely sensing that something may be wrong, never stopping long enough to search for a cause, let alone seriously considering a remedy. Years later, with 20/20 hindsight and a twinge of bitterness, they discover what should have been apparent at the time: that the job they held for seven years had become a dead end after three, or that they were never really comfortable in the job, or that they could have anticipated the downsizing that occurred.

What changes do you foresee in the decade ahead?

"Two major changes. Lifelong education is imperative. Continue the education process, acquire more usable knowledge, become more efficient intellectually, and accept the responsibility for building your financial security. Employers will be less and less able to afford medical and retirement benefits as we currently know them."
• C. E. Wild, Vice President, Human Resources, Ball Corporation

---

Okay, How Do I Begin Self-Assessment?

Let's start with an assignment that can serve you in a number of different ways. The following group of exercises will help you identify a whole range of likes, dislikes, strengths, and interests. For the most

"I swear, Mr. Winslow, this is the first 'personality profile' we've ever gotten back stamped *couldn't find one.*"

part, people tend to do best what they best like to do. The purpose of these exercises is to help you gain personal insight into what it is that you best like to do. In other words, these exercises will help you identify your "satisfiers" the elements that must be present in a future job if you are going to be comfortable and productive

Exercise One

Likes & Buts

In this exercise, we want you to list all the activities that you enjoy or find satisfying in your work. At the same time, we want you to counter each pleasurable activity with one that produces the opposite effect. For example: "I like selling in-person, but I hate selling over the telephone." Or "I like working with numbers and analyzing things, but I hate noise and commotion around me." Try to come up with as many examples as possible.

1. I like to _____
   But I _____

2. I like to _____
   But I _____

3. I like to _____
   But I _____

4. I like to _____
   But I _____

5. I like to _____
   But I _____

6. I like to _____
   But I _____

7. I like to _____
   But I _____

8. I like to _____
   But I _____

9. I like to _____
   But I _____

10. I like to _____
    But I _____

Exercise Two

What Did You Like Best . . .

. . . about your last (or present) job? In this exercise simply identify those aspects of your current or most recent job that you enjoyed the most. Think in terms of general responsibilities and areas of accountability.

_____

_____

_____

_____

_____

_____

_____

_____

Exercise Three

What's Been the Best So Far?

Try to describe the most satisfying position you have ever had. What made the job special? Think in terms of relationships, challenges, environment or company culture, rewards, etc.

_____

_____

_____

_____

_____

_____

_____

Exercise Four

All Work and No Play

What do you like to do during your non-working hours? Gardening? Maybe you're an artist and enjoy sketching? Or building things? Describe all of the activities that give you pleasure during your personal free time. This exercise will give you an idea of the skills you most enjoy using.

_____

_____

_____

_____

_____

_____

_____

Exercise Five

What's On Your Mind?

What do you read and talk about? List the magazines that you read most frequently. How about books? Can you recall the last five titles you've read? What do you talk about most with your friends, business associates, and family?

_____

_____

_____

_____

_____

_____

_____

Exercise Six

Let's Get Personal

Don't be modest. We want you to list the major personal qualities that you admire about yourself, especially in your work life. Here are some cues to get you started: *dependable, calm, professional, resourceful, steadfast, even-tempered, responsible, cooperative, loyal, patient, deliberate, perceptive,* etc.

_____

_____

_____

_____

_____

_____

Exercise Seven

Digging for Strengths

Now, consider your talents and abilities. List as many as you can that contribute to your success on the job. For example: *good with numbers, quick-witted, strong memory, cut through problems easily, strong leader, good writer, creative, persuasive, analytical,* etc.

_____

_____

_____

_____

_____

_____

Exercise Eight

How Do *They* See You?

Now that you have identified your qualities and talents, as *you* see them, let's put the shoe on the other foot. In your work experience, what are the qualities and talents that you believe *others* see in you?

_____

_____

_____

_____

_____

Exercise Nine

Let's Look at the "Down" Side

Just so you don't get overly confident, take a moment now to list all of the qualities or characteristics that you believe limit, or could limit, your career potential. Come on, now—you've got some, so think about it and list them!

_____

_____

_____

_____

_____

Identify My Accomplishments?
That Shouldn't Take Long.

Don't be so sure. You've probably accomplished much more than you suspect. Many of your achievements may not have seemed important at the time, but under closer examination they can reveal a great deal about your personal strengths and special skills. We are not talking about memorable, once-in-a-lifetime accomplishments. We want you to consider your career and work history in terms of the tasks you have faced and the results you have achieved.

How can any candidate maximize his or her chances of being hired?

"**Be able to show** results and accomplishments clearly. Show high energy, willingness to do what it takes, flexibility."
  • M. Jennings, Senior Vice President/Personnel, Gannett Company

---

How Can Past Accomplishments Help Me Now?

Besides being a good indicator of personal skills, a review of your accomplishments will play a major role in the shaping of your resume. Of all the basic elements found in a resume, none has more potential impact than your accomplishment statements. These are the brief one- to two-line attention getters that say: "Look what I've done before. I can do the same for you!"

This exercise also has other benefits. A thoughtful re-examination of your career will be extremely valuable when you reach the interview stage and must be able to speak freely and effectively about yourself. Having recently reviewed your past responsibilities and accomplishments, you will be much better prepared to apply your own experience and problem-solving abilities to meet the specific needs of a potential employer.

What Exactly Do You Consider an Accomplishment?

Broadly speaking, your accomplishments include the successful completion of just about any work-related assignment or task that clearly demonstrates a particular skill or combination of skills. Most impressive would be those in which you achieved something for the first time, exceeded past performance, or modified an existing procedure to the distinct advantage of your employer. But remember these accomplishments don't have to be earth-shaking. The fact that you reorganized a screwed-up filing system, for example, is clearly an accomplishment that could be used.

How Far Back Should I Go?

To the very beginning. Although the emphasis should be on your most recent job, don't ignore early positions and the tasks you successfully performed. Sometimes an early accomplishment can demonstrate a strength that has not been tested for many years.

The best way to approach this assignment is to start with your most recent job, then work backwards. Describe each position in terms of general responsibilities and accountabilities. What were the special problems you faced? How did you approach each problem, and what were the final results? Try to come up with at least *four* or *five* accomplishments for *each job* you've held.

Once your list is complete, go back over each accomplishment and try to identify the skills that were necessary to achieve your goal or task. Also try to quantify the results. For example, if you simplified a procedure, how many man-hours were saved by your innovation? In the next chapter ("How Do I Present Myself—The Resume"), we will discuss how to quantify your results and how to distill each accomplishment into a brief two- or three-line statement. For these exercises, however, don't hold back. Write down everything that comes to mind about the job and your accomplishments. In other words, don't try to edit your work here.

Exercise Ten

Identifying My Accomplishments

ACCOMPLISHMENTS IN MY MOST RECENT POSITION

    TITLE: _____

My work responsibilities were:

_____

_____

_____

What particular problems did I encounter?

_____

_____

_____

What actions did I take to solve the problems?

_____

_____

_____

The results of my actions were:

_____

_____

_____

What skills did I display?

_____

_____

_____

ACCOMPLISHMENTS IN MY PAST POSITIONS

TITLE: _____
My Work Responsibilities Were:

_____

_____

_____

What Particular Problems Did I Encounter?

_____

_____

_____

What Actions Did I Take to Solve the Problems?

_____

_____

_____

The Results of My Actions Were:

_____

_____

_____

What Skills Did I Display?

_____

_____

_____

Exercise Eleven

My Happy Sheet

In this exercise, you are being asked to prioritize the characteristics of a job that you believe must be present in order for you to be happy and productive.

This is a vitally important exercise, since the *top four* characteristics in each category *must* be present in the company you choose, its management, and in the position you occupy—if you're going to be happy and productive, that is.

Rank, in order of importance, the items in each of the categories below.

A. THE COMPANY

_____	1. Good image	_____	7. Lengthy business history
_____	2. Nationally-known products	_____	8. Promotes from within
_____	3. Single product or service	_____	9. Equal number of men and women in management
_____	4. Growth-oriented		
_____	5. Locally owned	_____	10. Size of company
_____	6. Located near my home		Small (25 to 150 people)

_____   Medium (150 to   _____   13. International lo-
               500)   cations
_____   Large (over 500)
_____   11. Superior bene-   _____   14. Leader in its
               fits   field
_____   12. Clearly defined   _____   15. Offers internal/
               management   external educa-
               policies   tional programs

B. THE MANAGEMENT

_____   1. Progressive   _____   8. Promotes em-
                                                 ployee incentive
_____   2. Participatory   programs
               style
                                     _____   9. Directed and fo-
_____   3. Conservative   cused on objec-
               and traditional   tives

_____   4. Highly struc-   _____   10. Strong sense of
               tured manage-   team spirit
               ment style
                                     _____   11. Dedicated to in-
_____   5. Flexible working   novation and
               hours   change

_____   6. Sense of humor   _____   12. Promotes atti-
                                                 tude of personal
_____   7. Frequent work   risk-taking
               reviews

C. THE POSITION

I need:
_____   1. To work inde-   _____   4. Freedom of
               pendently   expression

_____   2. Strong group   _____   5. Absolute control
               support   over job tasks

_____   3. To contribute
               new ideas   _____   6. Detail work

_____   7. Good advance-   _____   10. Opportunities to
              ment opportu-   gain prestige
              nity   and recognition

                                   _____   11. Challenging
_____   8. A warm and   work
              caring atmo-
              sphere   _____   12. To supervise and
                                                     influence others

_____   9. New projects   _____   13. Outlets for crea-
              available   tivity

                                   _____   14. To travel

Exercise Twelve

Management Styles

Describe the management styles of superiors for whom you have
worked.

A. STYLE I MOST ENJOYED, AND WHY.

_____

_____

_____

_____

_____

_____

B. STYLE I LEAST ENJOYED, AND WHY.

_____

_____

_____

_____

_____

_____

Now that I've Completed My Assessment Exercises—Whew!—How Do I Use Them?

To a large extent, you have already used them. By completing the exercises, you have given thought to a whole host of questions and subjects that, more than likely, you have ignored or taken for granted for years. It doesn't matter whether you've uncovered any surprises or simply reminded yourself of what you have known all along. What matters is that you have made a conscious effort to re-define yourself and to identify the complex combination of qualities that make you unique. Without this knowledge, especially as it applies to your career, you can easily stumble into the wrong job or an unhealthy situation. So, there's already been value received for your efforts. But don't stop there. Study your answers, and do some "threading."

Pet peeve concerning candidates?

"Candidates who do not know what they want to do. I am selecting for specific jobs, not career counseling."
   • John Regan, Corporate Employment Programs Manager, Digital Equipment Corporation

---

Threading? What's That?

Look for "threads" or common denominators in your exercise answers that can reveal a pattern, or a for a signal that says, "This is important!" For example, you may have expressed a preference for group activity. Okay, that's something to keep in mind. Then, upon closer study you discover you have also indicated that your most productive behavior results from an exchange of ideas and that working alone, isolated from your fellow workers, causes insecurity and discontent. Clearly, group activity no longer represents a simple preference; it has, by reinforcement, taken on the importance of an *essential* need and must be a major consideration when judging a job offer.

Don't I Need Help in Threading? Can I Really Do It Myself?

Although you can do much of the threading yourself, it's possible that an outside observer can do a better job. In other words, try to enlist the aid of a "third eye," someone who will study your answers with objectivity and look for the threads that you may have missed. We call this "partnering," and the partner you choose should be outside your immediate family because family members sometimes tend to be less objective than others and/or more emotional in their view of you. Perhaps a good friend who has your best interest at heart would be a good choice.

Can You Show Me How Threading Works?

Sure, but first we have to create a hypothetical case, so let's assume that these were some of your answers:

Exercise One ("Likes & Buts")
"I like to influence people and sell, but I hate office paperwork and reports."
Exercise Two ("What did you like best about your last job")
"The best thing about my last job was the freedom I was given— nobody breathing down my neck."
Exercise Three ("The best job you've ever had")
"We produced a terrific product, and I was given a lot of support from mangement when I needed it. The company also offered great incentives for goals met."
Exercise Four ("How you like to spend your spare time")
"I like theater and do a lot of acting in amateur plays."
Exercise Five ("What's on your mind?")
"I like politics, read and talk about it a lot."
Exercise Six ("Your personal qualities you most admire")
"My honesty, ethics, determination, and energy."
Exercise Seven ("Your talents and abilities")
"I'm persuasive, quick-witted, and can tell a pretty good joke."
Exercise Eight ("How others see you")
"They probably say I'm friendly and get along well with people,

that I'm a hard worker who puts in long hours, and that I know the product I sell."

Exercise Nine ("Your limitations")

"I'm not very good with numbers or detail. I also think office work is the pits."

Exercise Ten ("Accomplishments")

"I increased sales by twenty percent over a six-month period."

Exercise Eleven ("Your happy sheet"—Top four priorities)

> COMPANY: Nationally-known product, good image, growth-oriented, promotes from within
>
> MANAGEMENT: Flexible working hours, progressive, encourages risk-taking, provides back-up support
>
> POSITION: Independence, freedom of expression, challenging work, outlet for creativity

Exercise Twelve ("Management styles")

Management style you most enjoyed: "Easy-going, loose reins, supportive attitude."

Management style you least enjoyed: "Structured hours and work system, close supervision."

Okay, now let's see what kind of threads run throughout your answers.

It is pretty clear that sales, in one form or another, is your strong suit. Personal descriptors such as *influential, persuasive, friendly* (get along well with others), not to mention a talent for *acting*, all suggest important aspects of salesmanship.

Environmental threads must also be considered. Obviously, tight control is not something you appreciate or can adjust to easily. Words and phrases such as *freedom, independence, flexibility, easy-going,* and *loose reins* appear throughout your answers . . . too often not to be taken seriously.

Finally, an employer profile can be drawn from your answers. The company you work for must be a respected producer of a high-quality product or service. It should be progressive, in a growing phase, offer a strong dollar-incentive program, and provide opportunity for advancement. Your desire for a high degree of independence is well established, so the job must also support this need.

Once I Have Done My Threading, What Else Is Left?

Two final tasks. First, we want you to create your ideal job. In other words, if you had your druthers, how would you describe the job that satisfies all your needs? Don't be restrictive. Forget about reality for the moment. Let your imagination run wild, and think only about what, in your judgment, would constitute the perfect job.

Once you've completed a description of your ideal job, we'll move on to the next tasks, goal-setting and long-term planning.

What changes do you foresee in the decade ahead?

"**Less emphasis on career** or job-for-lifetime opportunities. More opportunities for short-run type employment. More requirement for mastery of specific new technology."
- Richard H. Hartzell, Manager, Corporate Human Resources, Sun Company

Exercise Thirteen
The Ideal Job, If You Had Your Druthers
Location:

_____

Industry:

_____

Your General Work Goal:

_____

_____

Type Of Company:

_____

_____

_____

_____

_____

A Description Of The Work Responsibilities You Would Like:

_____

_____

_____

_____

_____

Tangible Factors—types of job tasks you would like to perform:

_____

_____

_____

_____

_____

Intangible Factors—the environment you need for productive work:

_____

_____

_____

_____

_____

"Now that we've discussed your background—your B.A. from Vassar, your M.B.A. from Stanford—one final question: 'Can you type?'"

The knowledge gained through self-assessment is not of much value unless applied in a systematic way. Without a plan or a schedule to maintain, it is pretty easy to wake up one morning and discover that your career has been stalled or even derailed. If this comes as a complete surprise, it is fairly certain that you have not been paying attention—which brings us to the subject of career-planning and goal-setting.

Self-assessment is a collective process that goes far beyond an analysis of your strengths and weaknesses or your likes and dislikes. It also addresses the subject of career-planning and goal-setting, both

of which provide you with a structured means to monitor your progress and to warn you when something appears to have gone wrong.

What Exactly Do You Mean by Career-Goal-Setting, and How Does It Work?

The idea is to create an early-warning signal, an internal whisper (or
shout!) that says: "Hold it! This isn't working out as planned." But,
in order to be taken seriously, this warning signal must also provide
concrete evidence of problems, not just a feeling or suspicion that can
be easily ignored. We must have and see tangible evidence that there
is cause for alarm and perhaps a need for corrective action or, at the
very least, a serious reappraisal. In a sense, you must build your own
alarm system.

How Do I Set Career Goals?

In much the same way you would chart your course if you were to
drive from Los Angeles to New York. Let's say you want to make it to
New York in six days. To do that, you will need to average about 500
miles a day, so you get out the road map and plan your route. First
night, Flagstaff, Arizona; second night, Amarillo, Texas; and so on,
straight across the country. What you've done is to establish not only
a route to your objective, New York City, but also a time frame that
includes check points along the way. If, for example, you don't get to
Amarillo on your second night, you will know immediately that you
are behind schedule, and you will either have to find a way to make
up for the lost mileage or readjust your schedule.

   Your career early-warning system follows this same logic. It is almost as simple as this: Where would you like to be in ten years, and
what series of two-year goals will lead you to that objective? If your
plan is realistic, you will have plenty of warning if and when something goes wrong.

   Without clearly defined goals and a precise timetable, you are, to a
large extent, leaving your career development to chance, just as if
you were to start your trip from Los Angeles to New York without
any planning of even a road map. You may eventually get there, but
the odds are that you will have traveled much farther and longer than
necessary.

Which skills should a young man or woman acquire to be competitive in the coming decade?

"1. Computer literacy.
  2. Receptiveness to change.
  3. Career planning.
The idea of remaining thirty years with one company is becoming increasingly anachronistic. A young man or woman should think in terms of maximizing career options in an ever-changing world."
> • Dr. Brad Smart, President, Smart & Associates, Inc.

How Can Anyone Plan Ten Years Into The Future?

Ten years may seem like a long way off, but it really isn't. Think back to something that happened ten years ago. Does it really seem like that much time has passed? Probably not. But time isn't the issue. What's important is that you make an effort to take control of your career. If you can't plan ten years ahead, then reduce the goal setting period to six, or four, or even two years.

By deciding on long-term goals, or destinations, you've created targets, something to shoot for. By placing those targets a number of years in the future, you've given yourself an opportunity to adjust to situations that are perhaps unpredictable today. By working backwards, in two year increments—setting intermediate goals which will be realized in the next two, four, six, and eight years—you'll have created a formalized structure, a series of stepping stones arranged in a logical and attainable progression, each one leading you closer to your ultimate long-range career goal.

What If My Goal Is To Become a CEO in Ten Years?

We wouldn't want to discourage you, but at the same time, this goal may not be realistic—unless you're in top management right now, or unless you plan to own your own business. Too many factors, most of which you can't control, influence the appointment of a CEO. If you're now in lower or middle management, a more reasonable ten year plan might be to guide your career through as many different departments of a company (i.e. sales, marketing, or finance) to prepare yourself as thoroughly as possible for a major leadership position—even CEO. After all, a CEO must have a working knowledge of *all* these functions.

What is your pet peeve concerning candidates you interview?

"A fresh graduate M. B. A. who wants $50,000 a year."
  • John L. Hanson, Vice President/Human Resources,
  Parker Hannifin Corporation

All of This Sounds Very Calculating. Shouldn't Life be More Spontaneous?

More spontaneous than what? Look, all the planning in the world can't guarantee a smooth ride or an unaltered course. You can, however, minimize the major surprises, especially when it comes to your career. Time is relentless. One day you are just beginning; the next day—or, so it seems—you are in mid-career. Without definite goals and a structured plan to support the achievement of these goals, you can easily become lulled into a false sense of security. When this happens, watch out!

Obviously, none of us can control the future with absolute certainty. We can, however, take a more active, thoughtful role in guiding our own lives. A constant awareness of where we are and where we would like to be is the best safeguard against disappointment and failure.

How Can I Figure Out My Long- and Short-Term Goals?

The best way we know of is the following exercise.

Exercise Fourteen
Identify Your Objectives

What are your objectives: professionally, personally, and financially?

Instructions: Begin with your long-term plan and work backwards to determine where you will need to be and what you will need to know in order to achieve your goals. You should aim high, but not so high as to be unattainable. You will note that we have asked you to consider four different categories: Lifestyle, Financial Objectives, Personal Improvement, and Career Objectives. All these categories are interrelated and, in one way or another, support one another.

TEN YEARS

Lifestyle:

_____

_____

Financial Objectives:

_____

_____

Personal Improvement:

_____

_____

Career Objectives:

_____

_____

EIGHT YEARS

Lifestyle:

_____

_____

Financial Objectives:

_____

_____

EIGHT YEARS (*continued*)
Personal Improvement:

_____

_____

Career Objectives:

_____

_____

SIX YEARS:
Lifestyle:

_____

_____

Financial Objectives:

_____

_____

Personal Improvement:

_____

_____

Career Objectives:

_____

_____

FOUR YEARS
Lifestyle:

_____

_____

Financial Objectives:

_____

_____

FOUR YEARS (*continued*)
Personal Improvement:

_____

_____

Career Objectives:

_____

_____

TWO YEARS
Lifestyle:

_____

_____

Financial Objectives:

_____

_____

Personal Improvement:

_____

_____

Career Objectives:

_____

_____

ONE YEAR
Lifestyle:

_____

_____

Financial Objectives:

_____

_____

ONE YEAR   (*continued*)

Personal Improvement:

_____

_____

Career Objectives:

_____

_____

Once I Have Established My Goals, How Often Should I Review Them?

At least once every six months, take your list of goals out of the drawer and see if you are "on plan." If you are—if it looks like your present employer will satisfy your goals—then stay. If not, get out! Don't let your plan stay in the drawer gathering dust; use it. Let's say, for example, that you are now on the accounting staff, and your plan calls for you to move up to Director of Accounting Systems, reporting to the Controller, in a two-year span of time. During the eighteenth month of your two-year plan, you had better decide whether that jump is possible. If not, start your job-search campaign, because it will probably take you at least six months to relocate to that new job at the higher level in another firm. Goal-setting this way will keep you "on plan."

In your every-six-month analysis, make a special effort to stay aware of what the future holds for your company and industry.

— Is your industry or firm suffering severe price erosion?

— Is there a chance your firm will be merged or acquired and will a merged corporation need two employees in your function?

— Is your industry waning or even disappearing?

Also, look at internal aspects of the organization.

— Are you blocked by your boss or his or her boss?

— Is there a political problem preventing you from moving up?

— Do you fail to match the corporate culture in your dress, education (sometimes particular schools are an issue), age, work habits, social habits, experience, visibility, or potential?

If you answer "yes" to any of these questions, begin packing your bags, my friend!

Most amusing experience?

"A candidate brought his lunch (Kentucky Fried Chicken) into a job interview and proceeded to munch away during the questions and answers. Another candidate brought his mother with him into the interview. Needless to say, mom did all the talking. Almost hired the mom!"
  • Denny Wheeler, Manager, Corporate Human Resources, B. F. Goodrich

---

In Addition to Assessing Myself, Should I Consider Outside Vocational Testing?

If you are motivated to pursue the self-assessment process further, we certainly will not discourage it. The more you can learn about yourself, the better equipped you will be to face the challenges of your career and of life in general.

The sources for personality, aptitude, and vocational interest testing are so extensive (there are several hundred of them) that it would be impossible to list them all here. However, most colleges and universities offer testing of this sort at a modest cost. Another source would be your state Employment Development Department. The reference department of your public library can also provide you with information about the various vocational testing instruments available to the general public.

What About Career Counselors? Should I See One?

Basically, career counselors are going to tell you exactly what we are telling you in this book, which you have already paid for. They are going to give you pretty much the same system, but you will have to pay a whole lot more—in fact, in some cases, several hundreds or thousands of dollars. Some of them will give you vocational as well as aptitude testing; some of them won't.

There are many honest, competent career counselors out there, but keep in mind that there are also plenty of frauds and charlatans as well. If you decide to see a career counselor, here are some steps you can take to protect yourself from an unscrupulous con artist.

1. Visit the offices of several career counselors before making a decision.
2. Leave your checkbook at home.
3. Remember, you are only going on a research expedition. Don't be "fast-talked" into signing anything until you have completed your research.
4. Ask about their program and system.
5. Find out what *they* do, and what *you* do. If they say they act in any capacity beyond that of coach, beware! Only *you* can make appointments and go on interviews. *You* must conduct the job search.
6. Find out if they guarantee their system. If so, how long will the system take to achieve results? (Don't expect them to pinpoint the day you will be back at work, but you can expect a reasonable estimate.) Is it a money-back guarantee?
7. Who will be your counselor? Insist on meeting and talking with that person. If you don't feel good about him or her, ask to see another counselor, or forget about it.
8. Find out how long that person has been a counselor.
9. What kind of success has he or she had? Ask for references.
10. How much of the counselor's time will you get?
11. How much will the service cost?
12. Check with the Better Business Bureau and the state Attorney General's office to find out if any complaints have been filed against the company.

What About Changing Industries? How Can I Do That in the Nineties?

By planning it! But it takes *planning your work* and *working your plan*. Most companies try to recruit people who have had previous experience in the *same* job. So, if you are changing industries, you may have a problem. In reality, what you want is your boss's job in another company, in another industry, with more responsibility and much more money. But that is not how corporate management thinks.

So, if you are thinking about changing industries, you are facing a more difficult task than if you were looking around in your current industry. It is a rare exception that someone can simply walk into a company in a completely different industry and be hired. Of course, as with everything else, there are exceptions. People in certain functions have an easier time making this transition than others.

For instance, a corporate treasurer can expect good industry transferability, since in any company and/or industry, treasurers work primarily with banks and other lending institutions. The language everyone speaks is almost always the same—the language of money. Other financial functions, such as accountants and controllers, have good transferability too. People in the human resources field have a better-than-average transferability, since many compensation, displacement, and recruiting methods are standardized throughout all industrial sectors. Legal affairs specialists frequently can transfer easily, as can specialists in advertising and public relations.

The key issues here are common language and network. The farther you go from your current industry, the less likely you are to speak the same language, the same industrial lingo of catch words and phrases. Also, the farther afield you go, the less likely you are to be able to network into opportunities in other industries. That is, you will know fewer people who will be aware of appropriate job openings for you. (See our chapter on networking.)

You *can*, however, transfer to another industry—if you plan your move, research where you want to go, and then carefully plan your campaign. Look at industries on either side of yours, that is, industries that are customers of yours and industries of which your industry is a customer. The language will be transferable, and so will your network of contacts.

If, for example, you work in the production department of a cosmetics company, you should look at your suppliers: the chemical, packaging, distribution, and equipment vendors with whom your firm deals. Also talk with your customers: the wholesale distributors

and/or retailers whom you supply. They all know your business and
speak your language. Ask them about opportunities. But first do
your research, and determine what *you* can do for *them*, not what
they can do for you. We will talk more about this process in our chap-
ters on networking, research, and interviewing.

In summary, the farther away you go from your industry, and its
suppliers and customers, the more difficult it will be for you to transfer to other industries—unless, of course, you are in the CEO's family.

**What are the most effective techniques for changing careers
or industries?**

"Career change requires a disciplined analysis of what skills at
the task level are used in each industry. Then market these skills
and not the industry."

> • C. E. Wild, Vice President/Human Resources,
>   Ball Corporation

"Changing industries is much easier than changing careers. If
you develop your professional skills, you should be able to take
those skills to any industry. If your skills are unique to one
particular industry, then the change is that much more difficult.
One must take personal inventory, assess one's accomplishments,
re-define goals, examine personal finances, and discuss with
family. Changing careers can be traumatic, without proper
preparation."

> • Michael Sweet, Director, Compensation,
>   Benefits, and Human Resources Systems,
>   Paramount Pictures Corporation

**What about moving from the public sector to the private
sector?**

"I have done quite a bit of career counseling with individuals
moving from the public sector to the private sector. General
advice is:

". . . And if you don't hear from us in a week, Winslow, keep on looking."

- Lay the ground work a year or two in advance by taking business courses and establishing a professional network in private industry.
- Downplay information that might intimidate ("managed $1.3 billion budget").

- Have resume prepared in business terminology, not using vocabulary endemic to a particular public function.
- Regularly glance through the *Wall Street Journal, Fortune, Forbes, Business Week,* etc."
    - Dr. Brad Smart, President, Smart & Associates, Inc.

Strategies for the 90s

We've Been Acquired! Now, What Do I Do?

So, you believed top management when they announced there would be no layoffs—and you stayed. Or, perhaps you ignored those rumors and press reports that your company would be merged, acquired, sold, or spun off.

Well, it has happened! You will now experience a corporate culture shift, a nice-sounding phrase for: "Look out, the ax-man cometh." And he or she may not think you fit the new culture.

It is likely that, since two or more companies are being combined, many job functions will suddenly have two or more people filling them. Who is going to prevail, you or the other person? Here are some tips to make sure it is you.

1. Act as though you had just joined the company. You have to prove yourself all over again.
2. Strut your stuff! Decisions about the new staff may be made quickly, and you can't afford to sit back and wait to see what you're offered—do, and you may be outmaneuvered.
3. Determine which culture will prevail (the acquiror or the acquiree), and adapt quickly—you may not have weeks or months. Despite management protestations about both firms' equality, one culture always prevails, one becoming a little more equal than the other.
4. Research the other firm. Talk with staff members from the other firm about its history and heroes. Make friends with these folks.
5. Work at your highest level of productivity. Be seen as someone they can't afford to let go.

The decade ahead will see:

"**change, change, and more change.** Companies must be international, fluid, and more flexible than heretofore. Candidates for employment should recognize that the jobs they are trained for and the companies they have to join are changing institutions. Job seekers must keep their skills up-to-date in order to keep abreast of a changing job scene."
  • R. B. Hennessy, Vice President/Human Resources, National Starch & Chemical

---

"**I see the nineties** as a major departure from previous times. The technical industries are maturing. Employees are frustrated at mergers, plant closings, and the general lack of loyalty displayed by employers. I see a trend to a more European style of job contracts."
  • Gary Bernard, Senior Vice President/Human Resources, Dataproducts Corporation

---

Strategies for the 90s

Advisors

Advisors will be a very important part of any career management program in the nineties. They will be your outside objective eyes that won't let you kid yourself. They will also see the forest when you are only seeing trees because you are too close to yourself and your issues. These are the folks who can give you constant perspective on yourself, your abilities, and your thinking. They will also help you recognize and fit into the new jobs emerging in the decade ahead and beyond.

You should have two sets of advisors, senior and peer, but both should be external to the company, since you won't want these discussions revealed to the organization.

Senior advisors are those with "more shoe leather on the street." They are older, wiser people whom you can trust. They have been around longer and usually have a broader perspective on things. A senior advisor might also be an external mentor who has your interests at heart and will help you in many ways beyond simple advice. Clearly, these senior advisors will be key players in your network, and you should keep your network of senior advisors current at all times.

Peer advisors are friends or close associates who share many of the same problems and frustrations as you. Together, you can help one another.

How can a candidate use your human resources department to the best advantage?

"Don't be a pest. Be honest. Have a good idea of what jobs they're really qualified for."

> • M. Jennings, Senior Vice President/Personnel,
>   Gannett Company

"Obtain information about the structure, goals, and marketing strategy of the company. Try to determine the image the company is trying to project."

> • Joe Wegener, Vice President/Personnel,
>   A. P. I. Alarm Systems

CHAPTER TWO

HOW DO I PRESENT MYSELF—THE RESUME

Of all the words in the job-search lexicon, resume is, without a doubt, the most universally familiar. Along with our Social Security number, our resume follows us from job to job throughout our career. It is our proud badge of achievement. Everybody has one, from the high school senior who spent a summer working for the local newspaper, to the CEO who has just been relieved of his job. For anyone looking for a job, the resume is as indispensable as a mechanic's tools.

Yet, despite its widespread use, the resume remains a confusing and commonly misunderstood document. It is a supporting player that is often pushed into a starring role. It can't land you a job, but it can lose you one. It comes in a variety of shapes, colors, and sizes—and shouldn't.

Years ago, when movement from job to job was relatively rare, a resume could be little more than a basic summary of your employment history. Today, it has become a sophisticated marketing tool and, as such, must meet certain standards—standards set not by committee, but by an evolutionary process fueled by an increasingly competitive job market. In other words, a poorly executed resume can place you at risk.

The answers we have provided to the following questions are not absolute because nothing about a resume is absolute, but they do reflect conventional wisdom and, therefore, represent the surest and safest road to follow.

How Long Should My Resume Be?

That depends on how much work experience you have had. A safe rule of thumb is: one page, acceptable; two pages, ideal; three pages, only when absolutely necessary. Keep in mind that a resume is a summary, not an autobiography. It's intended to be a short cut, a time-saver—not for you, but for the person reading it and, perhaps, doing the hiring.

Should I Mail Out a Lot of Resumes?

Not unless you're into wasting money. Ninety-nine percent of all unsolicited resumes end up in the waste basket.

Do you respond to, or take notice of, unsolicited letters and resumes? Are they a good idea?

"We respond to all—25,000 per year. But they are not a good idea. The chances of getting a job through unsolicited resumes are less than one percent."
• Chris Lardge, Manager, Employment, Chevron Corporation

When Should I Include a Resume? When I Write for an Interview?

Not even then, unless you are answering an ad that requires you to do so. In fact, you are almost always better off *not* including a resume with your letter. Companies use resumes to screen *out* candidates. Why give them that opportunity? As good as your record may be, some minor detail could be enough to disqualify you from consideration. At least in a face-to-face interview, you have a chance to sway opinion your way. Write a good solid self-marketing letter instead of sending a resume. (See chapter on self-marketing.)

"I have good news and bad news, Mr. Winslow. The bad news is that I can't hire you. The good news is that I've found a publisher for your resume."

Should I Include References on My Resume?

No. References generally come into play only after you have made a strong impression and you are seriously being considered for the job. Always be prepared with references, but do not volunteer this information. Wait to be asked.

What about a Photograph?

No. Even if you look like a movie star. It is just possible you might also bear a striking resemblance to one of the screener's least favorite relatives, and that could mean a strike-out for you.

How about Salary or Salary History?

Never! Previous salary is a card that should be kept hidden as long as possible and revealed *only* after every effort to sidestep the issue has been exhausted. If you do include salary history, you will either *over-*price yourself and not get the interview, or you will *under*price yourself and not get enough money—even though the job is budgeted higher and you are worth it!

Should I Include My Age?

Also negative. Age, like salary history, is a real Catch-22. You are almost certain to be either too young or too old in the eyes of the person reading your resume.

Should I Have My Resume Professionally Printed?

It is not absolutely necessary, but it is advisable. A resume that has been typeset and professionally printed will almost always look better than one that has been typed on a typewriter and photocopied. Call it a subtle edge, but any edge is worth considering.

In many cases, your resume will represent a first impression, and if that first one isn't good, there may not be a second. A neatly prepared resume, written in clear, concise language, suggests a thoughtful and well-organized individual—in short, a good candidate.

If you simply can't afford the cost of typesetting and printing, be sure to have your resume typed on a good-quality machine, one that strikes sharply and clearly, or have it word-processed. Then, have the resume photocopied on good-quality bond paper.

Before your resume goes to the printer or photocopier, be sure that it's been proofread at least four or five times. Typographical errors and misspellings can quickly undo all your other good efforts.

What about Colored Paper?

Bad news. White or off-white is the color of choice. A light beige or buff is also acceptable. Bright colors tend to dominate and distract from the printed word. Also, even though you might use them to attract the reader's attention, you may be making a statement about yourself that you don't intend. "Do it right and go with white."

I Have Been Told There Are Two Different Resume Formats. What Is the Difference, and How Do I Decide Which One To Use?

The two basic formats are the chronological style and the functional or skill-based style. At the end of the book you'll find samples of each style.

The chronological resume is arranged by date, beginning with your most recent employer, then working backwards. This format should be your choice if you are changing jobs within your industry, seeking upward mobility and/or more responsibility in a similar career path, or if you've had a steady work history with no glaring, inexplicable gaps.

On the other hand, if you are planning a career change, have a short or spotty work record, or want to highlight accomplishments, the functional or skill-based resume is probably the one for you. This format will allow you to stress transferable skills and play up your accomplishments, while, if necessary, playing down your lack of experience. One caution, however. If you use this format to cover up or disguise gaps in your work history, keep in mind that most personnel directors are sophisticated enough to recognize the camouflage, so always be prepared with a plausible explanation.

What's the first thing you look at—or for—on a resume?

"Accomplishments."
> • M. Jennings, Senior Vice President/Personnel, Gannett Company

---

• "Format and neatness.
• Summary of professional experience.

- *Results*/accomplishments."
  - Beverly Fuentes, Vice President/Staffing and Employment,
    Bank of America

What Should I Emphasize in My Resume and How Do I Do It?

To a prospective employer, the two most interesting elements of your resume will be your past accomplishments and the skills you used to get the desired results.

In the previous chapter we discussed your inventory of past accomplishments. Now let's examine how to fashion them for your resume.

Your statements must *grab* the reader. They must be crisp and to the point, the point being the bottom line, the results you achieved. In other words, what did you accomplish, and what was the benefit to the company? The end results, or bottom line, should, if possible, be expressed in a quantitative figure, even if that figure only represents an estimate or close approximation. For example:

- Restructured sale of limited partnership interest, creating a $450,000 profit.
- Cut annual audit costs by one-third.
- Identified new profit center, resulting in $175,000 of new business.
- Designed new paper-flow system, saving two man-hours per week.

Quantitative results pack a wallop and enhance your credibility. Always begin your accomplishment statement with an action verb. Avoid weak, overly general statements such as "I have good communications skills" or "I am strong on detail." A potential employer is interested only in results and wants to see concrete evidence of your ability to produce.

Once you have compiled your list of accomplishments, study and re-write them as often as necessary. The shorter the statement, the more powerful it will be. Finally, commit your accomplishments to memory. You will want to be able to draw upon them at will during an interview.

At the end of this chapter, we have included several more examples of accomplishment statements, as well as a glossary of action verbs.

What's the first thing you look at—or for—on a resume?

"**Is it well organized** and readable? There is limited time available to review fifty or 100 resumes. I look for verbs that tell of action taken, what the industry and product are, the technology you command, and education."
> • C. E. Wild, Vice President/Human Resources
>   Ball Corporation

"**Clarity**—how quickly I can tell what the candidate's background really is."
> • Peggy Foster, Human Resources Consultant

Why Do I Need To Go Into Detail about My Accomplishments—Isn't My Job Title Enough?

Titles can be very misleading to the reader. Responsibilities can vary with the same title from company to company, as well as from industry to industry. No two organizations are structured alike, with the same responsibilities given to a specific title holder. The key here is to focus on accomplishments and responsibilities, rather than a specific title.

For instance, a fellow we know runs a large paper mill in a southwestern state. The mill produces about $200 million in annual sales volume. Our friend who runs the mill has the title of plant manager. Now, another friend of ours is in charge of manufacturing at a much smaller firm making computer software. The asset value of this firm is perhaps $1 million and sales volume is only $500,000 annually. His title is vice president of operations.

The difference in responsibility between the two is enormous, and yet the man with much less responsibility has the better title, vice president.

So, delineate your responsibilities—and accomplishments—particularly when your title doesn't truly reflect what you have been doing.

Do I Need an "Objective Statement" on My Resume?

Our feeling is that it is unnecessary and even a bit risky to include an objective statement on your resume, because it tends to narrow you too much. That narrowing could exclude you from situations you haven't even thought about. An objective statement belongs on your self-marketing letters, which focus on specific jobs.

Instead of an objective statement, put your professional and personal "footprint" at the beginning of the resume. The professional footprint is a brief summary of what you have done in your career. The personal footprint summarizes your style—*how* you did what you did.

An objective statement is:

"**Unnecessary unless the** candidate is targeting a specific employer for a specific job. I prefer a summary statement, positioned at the top of the resume, that briefly reviews career highlights."

- **Diane Briggs, Senior Employment Specialist, Digital Equipment Corporation**

I Am Interested in Two Career Directions— How about Having Two Different Resumes?

One hundred percent negative! As sure as you are reading this, you will run into someone who received *both* of your resumes, one received from you and the other from someone else, perhaps a friend trying to do you a favor!

One example that comes to mind is a friend who insisted on writing two different resumes, one focused on sales and the other on public relations with an emphasis on writing articles for clients—clearly, two entirely different objectives. After two months of trying to see the president of a major advertising agency, he finally got an interview, only to have it canceled the day of the meeting. Eventually, word drifted back to him from inside the company that the president canceled because he had received *both* resumes and felt that the candidate was confused and hadn't decided upon his career direction.

Given a chance, Murphy's Law will always win!

If you have experience in two or more functions and want to explore job possibilities in all of them, use the functional or skill-based resume format, which will allow you to cover *all* of your functional skills. That way, you can address your different objectives in your cover letters and not confuse the marketplace with different resumes.

The first thing I look for on a resume is:

"**Education** and/or relevant experience. Also, whether the cover letter has been generically written or is company-specific."
- Denny Wheeler, Manager, Corporate Human Resources, B. F. Goodrich

"... **the position** the candidate is seeking. This should be set out very clearly."
- Thomas J. Haines, Corporate Director, Human Resources, Fairchild Industries, Inc.

Should I Use a Professional Resume Writer?

It depends on how good a writer you are. Remember, the resume writer is going to charge you by the hour. If you are not a very good writer, then this kind of a service can be helpful. But resume writers are not mind readers, so, before you go in, decide on what format you are going to use and review your employment history and accomplishments. Develop your objectives and, in general, be prepared with all the material necessary to create a winning resume.

Before you decide on one of these services, however, be sure to look at samples of their work. Better yet, get a friend who writes well to help you with your resume and cover letters—and save the money!

"A resume is not going to get you a job, but it will get you an interview. When I review resumes, I do it quickly, usually ten to fifteen seconds each. I then divide them into three categories: yes, no, and maybe. In reviewing the resumes for a specific position, I have to have a very good understanding of the position and, therefore, know what I'm looking for: the proper work history, time in a particular job, areas of expertise. If I see nothing within the ten-to-fifteen-second scan, it will go to the 'no' pile. If there is a possibility of an interesting background that will require further reading or involves a history I'm not sure of, it will go to the 'maybe' pile. If the skills and proper work history are there, they jump out even within five seconds to the 'yes' pile. Typically, less than fifteen percent are 'yes,' with a few more in the 'maybe' pile, but always well over fifty percent are easy 'no's.'"

> • Michael Sweet, Director, Compensation Benefits, and Human Resources Systems, Paramount Pictures Corporation

---

Sample "Accomplishment Statements"

- Reduced turnaround time from five to four days, increasing production by 10 percent.
- Trained 400 new employees in customer service and in secretarial and telephone procedure.
- Processed vendor and freight invoices for monthly payment.
- Designed new product, resulting in first-year net profit of $175,000.
- Obtained bids and contracts from outside service companies.
- Supervised and assigned secretarial pool numbering 45.
- Created award-winning ad campaign.

"How can I hire a man who misspells his own name?"

- Identified and opened new market for company sales, resulting in 25 percent increase in volume.
- Devised new filing system that increased office efficiency.

Glossary of Action Verbs

accelerated	broadened	conducted	delivered
accomplished	built	consolidated	developed
achieved	changed	controlled	devised
added	clarified	converted	demonstrated
analyzed	completed	coordinated	designed
approved	conceived	created	determined

directed	launched	resolved	traced
doubled	led	revised	tracked
earned	made	scheduled	traded
eliminated	maintained	selected	trained
established	managed	serviced	transferred
evaluated	motivated	set up	transformed
executed	negotiated	simplified	translated
expanded	operated	sold	trimmed
formulated	organized	solved	tripled
founded	performed	sparked	turned
generated	planned	staffed	uncovered
halved	prepared	started	unified
headed	processed	streamlined	unraveled
identified	programmed	strengthened	utilized
implemented	promoted	stressed	vacated
improved	proposed	stretched	verified
increased	provided	structured	widened
initiated	purchased	succeeded	withdrew
innovated	recommended	summarized	won
instituted	redesigned	superseded	worked
introduced	reduced	supervised	wrote
invented	researched	terminated	

See Appendix for sample resumes (pp. 195–214).

Strategies for the 90s

Beware Signs of Change

"The new source of power is not money in the hands of a few, but information in the hands of many. . . . We now mass-produce information the way we used to mass-produce cars."

• John Naisbitt, *Megatrends*

Taking charge of your career in the nineties will mean staying aware of issues and changes around you that will affect it.

A change that would wreak havoc with your career is a change in CEO, if, that is, you're in the first three management levels below that office. A new CEO nearly always wants his or her own team, not a predecessor's—and that team also has their favorites. So, take heed if you're placed near a CEO and you smell a storm brewing. Better crank up your campaign quickly before you're cranked out.

The same basic principle applies to a change of boss at any level. The difference is that a change in CEO will frequently affect the ranks much more broadly and deeply than will changes in lower-level managers.

We're also constantly amazed at the number of people who see, hear—and, in fact, know—that a merger, acquisition, and/or downsizing is imminent, and yet DO ABSOLUTELY NOTHING TO GET OUT BEFORE THE AX FALLS. Top management, of course, always tries to allay fears and potential defections with all kinds of statements to reassure employees of their continued status. And it seems that these tactics work because, inevitably, so many employees end up staying—and are then displaced. We continually hear, "I didn't think it would happen to me."

Take control of your career! Wake up! Be aware! Look around! See what's happening! We're going to see enormous corporate change as we move through the nineties.

What changes do you foresee in the decade ahead?

"**Demographics** indicate a declining labor force; therefore, the *highly qualified* job-seeker can become much more selective in career choice."

- James E. McElwain, Vice President, Personnel Resources, NCR Corporation

"**In the coming decade,** the obvious skills are going to be related to the use of the personal computer and to the extent to which the personal computer continues its evolution. A second set of skills has to do with the ability to work within the 'political' system to obtain the most favored result for your project. (The ability to convince!)"

- **Russ Ringl, Corporate Director, Human Resources, American Medical Transport, Inc.**

Strategies for the 90s

What About Big vs. Medium vs. Small in the Nineties?

Well, in our view, the choice of corporate size depends on where you are in your career and how old you are. There is not an ideal size. The small companies are always trying to stay alive and grow into medium-sized companies. The medium-sized are trying to organize, systemize, and energize so they can become large. The large ones are trying to regain what they had when they were medium-sized—a sense of family, unity, responsiveness, flexibility, and spirit.

So, let's look at what each size will and will not offer for the decade ahead.

Biggies

Big companies are generally well-known. They are slow to move and respond, because decisions need multiple approvals. They are bureaucratic, with complex systems, procedures, and politics. This is where politics is an art form. The power here is usually at much higher levels than is necessary. Financial, technical, and human resources are usually extensive, but they are difficult to rally because of bureaucracy, politics, and the approval process.

It is always to your advantage to have *been* with a large firm (not necessarily to *be* with one). Therefore, we suggest that experience with a large company is usually a very good move early in a career. You can move on to a small or medium-sized organization for a time and then—if the right opportunity surfaces—go *back* to the large company. You frequently can jump to a higher level upon returning to a large company than you could if you'd stayed there all along.

Remember that long careers in big companies carry long odds for reaching the top. There is only one CEO (or even CFO or COO) but an enormous number of people below him or her. To stay here means you must play politics well, and you must stay visible (create projects, make public speeches, and write articles—get out there and let them know you're around).

Middlers

It has been said that medium-sized companies offer the best of all worlds. There is financial stability here, but also creativity and individuality. Here you can be more effective as an individual. There are not as many bureaucratic systems and procedures, nor as many approvals needed to do something. There is also frequently more potential for you to be visible to senior management. However, before you commit to a mid-sized company, be sure you've checked out their product or service, the ownership situation (if it's a family-owned place, stay out of it unless you get an iron-clad contract), as well as the corporate culture (the environment and the people with whom you would be working).

One bit of caution: depending on all sorts of variables, of course, the mid-sized company is frequently the target for takeover by larger sized companies. And guess whose job may be out the door!

Half-Pints and Start-Ups

Small companies are risky, so your commitment to them should be shorter (at least initially) and the payoff should come faster. Unless you are simply in it for the creative ride, the pay should be better than at the larger firms and a piece of the action is a *must* (either stock or considerable profit percentages). Make sure that you get the deal in writing and that it contains an exit policy in full detail.

If you choose a small company or a start-up, choose one in a business about which you know something. That way, you won't have a long learning curve, and you can begin to make a contribution earlier (so you won't be a drag on the finances). Also remember that small and start-up companies live or die rapidly on their customer bases.

Now, now, Mr. Winslow, don't take it so hard. It was a lousy job to begin with."

Although manufacturing and operations are important, sales and marketing expertise is vital—or the outfit won't be around long. So, be sure about who is in the "selling seat" and what their track record is.

How can a candidate use the human resources department to best advantage?

"**During initial interviewing,** probe the H. R. person regarding the hiring manager's style—philosophy, goals, etc.—to be better

prepared for the interview. Candidates are usually so busy
answering questions to validate their own credentials that they
fail to be aggressive enough in finding out about the person and
function who will be interviewing them and making the hiring
decision."

- Vera Blanchet, Vice President/Human Resources, Corporate
  Headquarters, California Savings & Loan Association

How to maximize your chances of being hired,

"**know something about the company** and the position in
advance so you can better demonstrate to the individuals having
the authority to hire how your background and skills fit the
needs of the position they are looking to fill. Be enthusiastic in
presenting yourself and your qualifications. Demonstrate how
you can help fill the needs and solve the problems unique to their
position."

- James J. Carter, Principal, Avery Crafts Associates Ltd.

My pet peeve is:

"**well-educated candidates** who don't know how to listen and
communicate. What a waste."

- Denny Wheeler, Manager, Corporate Human Resources,
  B. F. Goodrich

CHAPTER THREE

WHERE THE JOBS ARE—
AND HOW TO FIND THEM

Jobs—they're everywhere! Newspapers, magazines, employment agencies, storefront windows. Good times or bad, there are always jobs to be filled. Of course, most of these jobs wouldn't interest you. And those that would seem to interest hundreds of others as well.

That's the bad news. The good news is that the *publicly advertised* job market represents the tip of the iceberg—by some estimates, less than fifteen percent of the entire job market at any given time. Get the picture? That's right; it is estimated that up to eighty-five percent of the available jobs are never publicly announced, and it's this hidden job market that you have to penetrate if you want to swing the odds in your favor.

Aren't All Job Openings Publicly Announced?

Absolutely not! In fact, the vast majority of job openings are filled without ever being revealed to the public at large.

Why is That?

For a variety of reasons. Many companies prefer to promote or fill a vacancy from within the organization. Other companies may simply want to avoid the rush of resumes that come in when a job opening is advertised, not to mention the time-consuming procedure of inter-viewing that must follow. Economics may play a role. If, for example, the filling of a vacancy is farmed out to an executive search firm or employment agency, the company will have to pay a fee if it hires someone sent by either of these sources.

If Most Job Openings Aren't Advertised or Publicly Announced, How Can I Find Out about Them?

Basically, there are only two ways. One way is to make "cold" con-tact with a company in your field, either by phone or letter. The other technique is far and away the most efficient and effective means of penetrating the hidden job market. It is called *networking*.

Networking? What Exactly Does that Word Mean?

In simplest terms, networking is the technique of utilizing other people or contacts to help you find a job. One person introduces you to another who introduces you to three others. It is an extremely powerful process.

"Networking is an extremely valuable tool in locating a new position and helping each other out in day-to-day activities. When networking, don't overlook anyone; the contacts you don't think can help are many times your most valuable, both today and tomorrow."
> • Russ Ringl, Corporate Director, Human Resources, American Medical Transport, Inc.

But People Aren't Going To Want To Talk to Me or Help Me. They Are Probably Too Busy, Right?

Wrong! Networking is partly based on the premise that most people actually like to be asked for advice and counsel. They like to be thought of as *experts*. And, when you get that job they suggested or introduced you to, watch out! Just stand back and listen to them tell you and others how they were responsible for your job success. And that's just fine with you, right? After all, *you* have the job.

But What If I Don't Have any Contacts?

Oh yes you do! You have contacts you haven't even met yet. The reason you think you are short on contacts is that you are thinking only in terms of so-called important or influential people: decision-makers, etc. You will reach those people eventually, but first, you have to start thinking about who you *do* know, regardless of whether they have any connection with your line of work. Your family doctor, for example, might lead you to a job opening.

How Can My Family Doctor Help Me Find a Job?

Think for a minute about how many people your doctor knows. He or she has a huge list of patients as well as professional associates. To illustrate the point, let's create a scenario. We will assume that you are an unemployed loan officer, and your family doctor, old Doc Bradley, has a large practice and many friends, one of whom happens to be his fishing buddy, Tom Worthalot, President of United Savings and Loan. When Doc Bradley learns of your situation (you have told him, of course), he wants to help and offers to call Worthalot on your behalf. You follow up on his introduction a few days later, and an interview is arranged.

Now you are on your own, but what's important is that you have gotten in to see someone whom you wouldn't normally be able to reach. If all goes well, you will make a good impression, and, if the timing is right, you may have walked into an unadvertised job opportunity that is a perfect match. Or, if you have really done your homework and come in prepared with some creative ideas, who knows, Worthalot might even create a job for you.

Regardless of the outcome, you are ahead of the game. Even if there aren't any current openings, you have made a good impression and will be remembered when a job vacancy does occur. It is also possible that Worthalot, though unable to hire you, is sufficiently impressed to make a few phone calls on your behalf. Now your network is really cooking! Worthalot's recommendation obviously carries a lot of weight, and your job search is moving into high gear—all because of help from an unlikely source, your family doctor.

Isn't There a Lot of Luck Involved in Networking?

Yes and no. If Doc Bradley was the only person you contacted, then you could chalk it up to luck. But that's not the way to network effectively. You are involved in a numbers game, and the greater the numbers, the better your chances of uncovering legitimate job leads.

In What Way Is Networking a Numbers Game?

Basic common sense. Twenty people can cover a wider area than five. The more people you enlist in your job search, the greater your chances of penetrating the hidden job market, that unpublished market with up to eighty-five percent of the available jobs. Ideally, your network should grow like a chain letter, each new contact leading to two or three others, and so on.

How Do I Begin Building a Network?

The first step is to compile a list of everyone you know, and we mean *everyone*. Get out your black book and Christmas card list. Don't be judgmental at this stage. If you know someone well enough to call on the phone or to meet with in person, put his or her name on the list.

Your list should include friends, relatives, church members, former employers and co-workers, your former boss, your dentist, banker, real estate broker, insurance broker, lawyer, accountant, and service professional with whom you do business, customers, suppliers, and local merchants such as your grocer, butcher, jeweler, and even your barber or hairdresser.

Just like Doc Bradley, these people have friends, clients, and associates and may be able to suggest other people for you to meet. Other good sources for initial contacts include alumni associations, former teachers, professional or trade organizations, clubs, civic groups, and the local Chamber of Commerce.

Remember that as well as you know someone, you can't possibly know all of *their* friends and associates. Your cousin Larry may have gone to school with someone who is now in a position to help you, or he may know someone who knows someone whom you should meet. And here is a nifty idea: look over your checkbook for the past year. We'll bet you will find a few network contacts there!

Do I Really Have To Tell All These People that I Am Out of Work and Looking for a Job?

Only if you want them to help. Look, there is no reason to be ashamed or self-conscious about being unemployed or about wanting to change jobs. In today's business climate, it is a rarity to find anyone who has been with a company more than four or five years. Basically, people *want* to help, and you will find that most people will be understanding and sensitive to your needs. Some will have had similar experiences; others will know that one day they may be in the same position as you. Although few will expect you to say so, make it clear that if they ever need your help, you will be there to return the favor.

When I Speak with My Network and Possible Employers, How Should I Explain My Unemployment?

Well, that depends on why you are unemployed, of course. Did you quit? Were you fired? Were you laid off in a downsizing? The key here is consistency. You must say the same thing that others will say about why you are unemployed—the same thing as your former boss, the personnel department, and the co-workers who might be called as references at your former company.

The last thing you want is to say one thing and have others say something else. That is really bad for your credibility. Obviously, if you are unemployed for reasons other than firing, then simply be honest and explain the circumstances. On the other hand, if you were fired from your last job, the best thing to do (even if it hurts) is to go back to your boss, or whomever fired you, and tell that person you need a credible story about what happened.

If your departure from the company was particularly bitter, we suggest you meet first with someone in personnel and explain the dilemma you are facing: that you simply can't go around to potential employers telling them that you were fired from your last job. It is in no one's best interest, least of all your former employer's, to see you without a job for an extended period of time.

Try to use the personnel department as an ombudsman. See if you can't get them to agree upon some less damaging reason for your leaving. Some suggestions might be: "difference in management style," "personality conflict," "limited opportunity for personal growth," or even "position eliminated."

Let the personnel department handle your former boss, but be certain that everyone agrees on a single story before you use it. Then make sure that anyone else who might be called as a reference is clued in. Remember, a seasoned reference-caller knows how to ask for one person's comments and then ask whom else to talk to in the company; they know how to network too!

It is a good idea to write out your agreed-upon story and give a copy to each person who might be called. Suggest that everyone file the story in a convenient place. That way, when a reference call comes in, everyone can simply go to the file and quickly retrieve it to refresh their memories as to what to say. Don't forget—it is essential that everyone have a consistent story.

How can a candidate use your human resources department to the best advantage?

"Use of the human resources department gives the candidate widest possible consideration by all parts of the corporation that are actively hiring. Use of the H. R. system allows H. R. to monitor all open jobs within the corporation."

  • Chris Lardge, Manager, Employment, Chevron Corporation

Once I Have a Large List of Network Names, What Do I Do?

This first list is your direct list: those whom you know and with whom you are reasonably comfortable. Prioritize the list. You may have too many names to approach at the same time, so it is important that you look at each name in terms of (1) how well you know the person, (2) how willing he or she may be to offer assistance, and (3) how helpful that assistance is likely to be. The third question is tough to answer because good contacts often come from unexpected sources.

Create a direct-contact "A" list of those people you feel will help the most, and then create a "B" list of those less likely to help. Begin by contacting the names on your "A" list. Eventually, you will get around to your "B" list and, when you do, don't be surprised if someone from this list becomes the most helpful of all—it happens all the time. So DON'T ELIMINATE ANYBODY! Put everybody on either the "A" or "B" list. Frequently, the person who you think won't do anything *really surprises you.*

When you first make contact, be candid about what has happened, and be sure to make it clear that you are *not* asking for a job. You don't want to put anyone in the embarrassing position of feeling that they have let you down because they can't offer you a job. All you are looking for is ideas, references, introductions, or job leads. If the person you are contacting happens to be in the same field as you, indicate that advice on marketing strategy would be appreciated as well.

What Should I Say When I First Contact these People?

For these direct contacts (those whom you know well) simply follow these steps:

1. Tell them you are involved in a job-search campaign and would like to discuss why you are leaving or have left your current job. Always indicate that your overall objective and the reason you are talking with them is a search for better opportunities.

2. Re-acquaint them with your background and describe the type of job you want.

3. Try to make them feel comfortable about you and your search. Although you may have known many of these people for a long time, chances are they are not fully informed about your career, so it is important that you discuss your expertise: your problem-solving abilities, as well as your skills and experience (all this from your resume). Once they are reassured that you are a good, solid job candidate and won't embarrass them, they will be more than willing to introduce you to their friends and associates.

4. Mention your target companies (see chapter four: "What's Out There—Researching the Job Market") and, if possible, name the people within those companies whom you would like to meet. Here is where research pays off. Ask if your network contact knows any of these people or if someone else whom he or she knows might know them. The fact is, your network contacts are not mind-readers. You have to guide them, tell them what you want them to do. How much more effective it is to say, "Do you happen to know Long John Plunger at Cloggo Plumbing?" or "Do you know Dorothy Starmaker at Acme Entertainment?" than simply to ask, "Do you know of any jobs?" You have to focus and lead your network by identifying your target companies and the decision-makers whom you want to meet within those companies. This way, the process will be so much more effective.

5. If they don't know anyone at your prime targets, don't be shy: ask for other suggestions. Now that they understand the kind of job you want, they will be much more able to help.

6. When a contact mentions someone you should meet, ask for an introduction. If that creates some hesitancy, ask if you could simply use their name as a referral introduction. This is usually no problem.

7. Be sure to leave extra copies of your resume. You never know whom they will have lunch with tomorrow or play golf with on Saturday. We have known many introductions made (and jobs later offered) by one person mentioning an open position to a friend over lunch or on the golf course or tennis court.

8. Always remember to send a thank-you note after each network contact you make. This is not only good manners, it also keeps your name in front of your network.

9. Follow up in a couple of weeks, just as a reminder. Remember,

"Mr. Winslow, I respect your desire to bring peace and harmony to a troubled world, but are you sure *Consolidated Armaments* is where you want to begin?"

your picture is probably not on their desk, so "out of sight, out of mind."

How Should I Handle the Referrals I Get Through My Direct Network of Friends?

The people to whom you are referred by your direct network are the people who make up your indirect list, and the next stage of the networking process works pretty much the same way as we have just described, with a few minor differences.

By this time, your direct contacts will have begun offering suggestions and providing introductions, and you will have become more comfortable with the networking process. This should make it a lot easier for you to talk with strangers. But remember, these folks aren't psychic either. You have to tell them what you want, just as you did with your direct contacts.

These indirect network contacts may be in the industry or company you want to enter, so here are a few additional things you will want to do:

1. Be sure to begin your letter or phone call by saying, "Our mutual friend _____suggested I contact you." Now, the reason for this is not as obvious as it may seem. Sure, it is an easy way to begin a letter or phone call, but, more importantly, it is the best way to get through the secretary. A secretary is not likely to sidetrack your letter or call if there is a possibility that the boss's friend might find out.

2. Of course, try to get an appointment to see your indirect contacts. When you do, request that they review your resume and suggest how it could be improved. Even if you can't get an appointment, send a resume and request suggestions. At least then, you can be fairly certain that your resume has been read and that your contact is familiar with it.

3. Whether in person or on the phone, discuss your job campaign strategy and ask for a critique of it. Again, *everyone* likes to be asked for advice and counsel.

4. Discuss their industry (and maybe their company, but be careful not to ask for a job) with an eye toward *opportunities*.

5. Try to identify problems you can solve in their industry or company. Mention what you have discovered in your research and ask for confirmation of this information.

6. Ask for names of companies and people that this person can suggest you contact (and maybe even introduce you to!). You will, of course, want to ask this question *after* you have discussed *your* target list (from your research).

7. Make sure you follow up with a thank-you letter.

8. Don't forget to continue following up by phone and letter. Remember, "out of sight, out of mind."

Aren't My Contacts Going To Get Awfully Tired of Hearing from Me?

It depends on how it's done. As long as you are not overbearing and don't give the impression that your contact is somehow committed to help, you will find that most professionals admire and appreciate persistence. They recognize persistence as a necessary ingredient of success. You must, however, be sensitive to their needs as well. If you phone and sense that you have picked the wrong time, apologize and sign off quickly. Then try again later.

Here's a neat trick that can be a winner if handled properly. Instead of phoning three or four times in succession, try sending a particularly funny cartoon from the newspaper or a magazine like the *New Yorker,* along with a short note to keep them abreast of your job campaign. The cartoon (best if it has some genuine meaning for your contact) will brighten what might otherwise be a dull, drab morning, and the note will be an *unpressured* reminder of your availability.

What is your pet peeve concerning candidates you interview?

"Apathy—a 'what have you got?' attitude."
  • **Richard H. Hartzell, Manager, Corporate Human Resources, Sun Company**

What are the Drawbacks of Networking?

We have never encountered any. All you are doing is fishing with a net instead of a single line. Your task is to penetrate the hidden job market, which, as we have already pointed out, is where a large majority of the available jobs exist. Without insider knowledge of these jobs, your chances of stumbling onto one is minimal. With the assistance of a growing network, your chances improve tremendously.

Is There Some Special Way To Keep Track of My Network and All the Referrals?

A good question. It is of critical importance that you know whom you have contacted, as well as when, and, in the case of an indirect contact, who was responsible for the introduction. Unless you have easy access to this information, you will find yourself making embarrassing mistakes, failing to follow up promptly, and in general undermining your networking efforts.

Here is a simple but effective means of keeping track of your network. It is a network inventory that can be maintained on 3" × 5" cards or in a looseleaf notebook. If you use this system, it is vital that you create a new network inventory card for *every* contact.

NETWORK INVENTORY CARD

NAME _____TITLE _____

COMPANY _____

ADDRESS _____

CITY, STATE, ZIP _____

COMPANY PHONE _____

SECRETARY'S NAME _____

RELATIONSHIP/REFERRAL:

ACTION TAKEN:

REFERRED TO:

Use the reverse side of the card for contact's biographical information such as:

- wife's or husband's name
- children's names
- clubs or social affiliations
- hobbies and/or sports enjoyed
- special interests
- career history
- home address and phone number

Obviously, Networking Is the Way To Go, but Are You Suggesting that I Not Bother with Want Ads?

Not at all. Let's face it, it doesn't matter *how* you find a job, as long as you find one. All we are saying is that the vast majority of jobs are found through networking and/or direct company contact. If you doubt this, simply ask a group of your friends how they found their jobs. Chances are, most will respond with something like, "Oh, I heard about the job through a friend of mine who was working for the company." If the success of your job search is contingent on published ads or on the efforts of executive search firms or employment agencies, you will find that you are playing the long odds instead of the short. By so doing, you will also increase your exposure to risk.

There Is a Risk to Using Want Ads?

Yes. It is the risk of being unemployed much longer than necessary and being forced to take a job that isn't to your liking. Sure, you have to explore every opportunity. That includes reading the want ads and contacting as many personnel agencies and search firms as possible, but if you are going to sit around and wait for someone else to find you the *perfect* job, you are likely to have a pretty long wait. *You* must take control of your job search! Concentrate your energy on the most efficient and productive means of finding a job—not the easiest.

Now, here is an example of what can frequently happen when you answer the want ad sweepstakes. A vice president of human resources for a large company recently decided to conduct a classified ad campaign to fill a vacancy for the post of regional sales manager. He ran his ad in the Wednesday and Thursday *Wall Street Journal* and in the Sunday edition of the *Los Angeles Times*, the *New York Times*, and the *Chicago Tribune*. Know how many responses he got? Over 3000! Granted, somebody is going to get the job. But against those odds, you would be better off putting your twenty-five cents of postage in a Las Vegas slot machine!

Do you use employment ads? Successfully? Why do so many employers fail even to acknowledge ad responses?

"Classified advertising is regularly used and continues to be productive for the majority of openings. Applicants expect to use the classified section, and it will be used until there is a more productive and visible process. Those employers who refuse to

answer all inquiries for employment are not committed to being a desirable or attractive employer and will be less competitive in a tight labor market."
• C. E. Wild, Vice President/Human Resources, Ball Corporation

Okay, But If I Spot a Job Ad That Looks Like a Good Fit, How Can I Get the Best Shot at It?

First, you have to realize what kind of situation you face. There may be hundreds, even thousands of responses coming in. Initially, they will be screened *not* by the person doing the hiring—oh, no—but most likely by an assistant in the personnel department, possibly stuck in a far corner at a card table, under poor lighting conditions. The screener *hates* the job and is thinking about that evening's date, or this morning's car trouble, or next week's vacation—everything BUT the stack of letters and resumes to be sifted through. And you are going to trust your job campaign to this environment?

Do you really think this bored, tired, uninterested screener cares one bit about you and your resume, especially if it is an eight-page autobiography? Do you really think it is going to be read with a mother's love and care? Of course not!

Additionally, there are usually two piles of resumes: a "yes" pile and a "no" pile. The "no" pile is huge and frequently dumped into "file thirteen" (you know, the large brown wastebasket that the cleaning crew empties each night).

But all is not lost. There *is* a way to catch the wandering eye (and mind) of this screener. The secret is to make the task easier.

Okay, how? First, you have to understand that taped to the desk or card table in the corner, with just enough light to be read, is a copy of the newspaper ad that describes the job requirements and the necessary experience, skills, etc. This information is what the screener is looking for in your cover letter and/or resume.

Notice, we said *cover letter!* This is important because your cover letter is the first thing a screener will see and, you hope, read. In fact, if properly written, it may be all that is necessary. You should try to imitate the ad in content and style. If the first requirement outlined in the ad is a Bachelor of Arts degree—and you have one—then lead off your letter with a mention of your B.A. degree. Carefully follow the sequence of the ad in your letter. By doing so, you will have made the screener's job easier and therefore considerably increased your chances of landing in the "yes" pile. In our chapter on self-marketing, you will find some examples of winning ad-response cover letters.

Now, here is a nifty method of by-passing the screening process entirely. It is possible, especially in large companies, that the name of the person in the ad to whom you're supposed to respond is actually an outside recruiter: a search firm or employment agency. Sometimes they are even fictitious names, keyed to indicate that you have answered an ad from one source (a particular newspaper) or another. You should try to circumvent this screening process if at all possible—and it is possible. Here's how. Use the research techniques found in the next chapter to do the following:

1. Look up the company in the appropriate directory (such as *Standard & Poors, Moody's,* etc.).
2. Discover the name of the senior person in your field. If you are in finance, for example, look for the V.P./finance.
3. Phone this individual.
4. Explain, without referring to the advertisement, that you understand they are looking for someone with your qualifications, and pursue the point to an interview invitation.

This direct approach has worked very effectively for many of our clients. It is certainly a lot better than the ad-answering lottery approach.

Don't forget that with a job search you are involved in an intelligence gathering operation. Don't be deterred by little roadblocks. We have a tendency to be put off too easily by the little detours others place in our way. The blind ad is one such item. These are the ads that make no mention of a company name, but request that you respond to a post office box number.

There are times when blind ads are valid and the company placing them simply does not want to be bothered with meeting a large group of job seekers. The problem is the company may *not* be one you want, or it may be one you would rather not know you are looking for a job—your current or most recent employer, for example.

Then too, many blind ads are not legitimate and do not represent an available job opening. They are often placed by job shops looking for resumes. They will file these resumes in their proper categories and then try to drum up business by sending them all over town. Now, you might think this is a terrific way to get leads, but it isn't, because you've lost control of your job campaign. In fact, it could spell disaster, especially if you are still employed and don't want your boss to find out you are looking. So, what can you do? How can you find out who placed the blind ad? Here is a technique that is often successful.

Let's assume you see an employment ad describing a position that fits your qualifications. No employer or company is identified in the ad. Instead, you are requested to respond to: P.O. Box 14523, Los Angeles, CA 90068. Here is what you can do:

1. Call the main post office in Los Angeles.
2. Ask what sub-station handles zip code 90068.
3. Call that sub-station and ask for the post office box manager. Now, explain to the manager that the ad is requesting a resume and that you would like to know the name of the box owner before responding. Explain that it may be your current employer, or one with whom you are now talking, and you would prefer that they didn't know you are answering the ad. Often the manager will be sympathetic and simply give you the information you need. At other times, it may take some additional pleading. In some cases, the manager will just refuse to release the information. Regardless of the outcome, it is always worth a try.
4. If you are successful, and the owner of the box number sounds like an agency or job shop, you might drive by and check them out. On the other hand, if the owner turns out to be a legitimate employer, you can then follow the same procedure we suggested for circumventing the screening

process (that is, contact the company directly, and speak specifically with the person who will be doing the hiring).

Finally, if your efforts to discover the owner of P.O. Box 14523 fail, and you are still worried about your resume falling into the wrong hands, send your resume and cover letter in one envelope and enclose *that* envelope within another, along with a letter addressed to the postmaster for the sub-station. That letter should clearly indicate that if the box number is owned by A., B., or C. company, you do *not* want the inside envelope delivered but instead returned to you.

Do you use employment ads? Successfully?

"We use general recruiting ads mostly. We use specific want ads for hard-to-fill openings only. They are expensive and generally we find a 1-in-500 to 1-in-1000 chance of developing qualified candidates."
 • Chris Lardge, Manager, Employment, Chevron Corporation

"Yes. Yes. Every company I've worked for acknowledged all solicited responses."
 • John J. Regan, Corporate Employment Programs Manager, Digital Equipment Corporation

Does Networking Mean I Should By-Pass the Personnel Department?

Not necessarily. Of course, you must understand that the personnel department (now frequently called human resources) does not actually make hiring decisions, except regarding personnel department employees. The hiring decisions are made by the line or staff managers responsible for whatever the newly hired person is to do. For example, the decision to hire a supervisor in production will be made by the production manager or perhaps by the vice president of manufacturing.

"Your job application seems to be in order, Miss Baxter. Now, may I see your teeth?"

The personnel department provides a screening mechanism through which many potential candidates can be found. The best of these applicants are then presented to the line manager, he or she making the choice about the final hiring.

Personnel can be very helpful to you, however. After all, these folks *do* have the ear of the company's managers. But, like everyone else, they are not mind readers; they don't know who you are, what you want to do, or what you *can* do. So, it is up to you to use the personnel people as you would any network contact. In other words, before you approach personnel, do your research, know about the company and its problems and then, if possible, overlay your abilities and experience on those problems. Personnel *will* be impressed and no doubt will make the appropriate introductions.

Is it risky to circumvent the human resources department?

"Not necessarily, but it depends on a person's skill in doing so. Most function heads will send resumes on to the H. R. function anyway. I would send a resume to *both* the function head and the H. R. department."
- Thomas J. Haines, Corporate Director, Human Resources, Fairchild Industries, Inc.

"It depends on the company, but generally I would say no. A top-notch candidate will be known by the H. R. group even if the candidate circumvents H. R."
- R. B. Hennessy, Vice President/Human Resources, National Starch & Chemical

"No risk—if you are highly qualified."
- John L. Hanson, Vice President/Human Resources, Parker Hannifin Corporation

Is It Possible To Create a Job for Myself?

You're darned right it is! It's done all the time. The issue here is awareness of your goals, strengths, and accomplishments, plus the degree of research you have done on a company.

If you know what you want, all you need is to do your research and find an organization that has a problem which *you* can solve. Network into the company, or even contact the person with the problem directly with a "broadcast" letter (see the self-marketing chapter for a discussion of the broadcast letter), and state your case.

Also bear in mind that companies are always looking for good talent. Even if there is not an immediate opening for your particular specialty, companies will frequently bring talented people on board with an eye to future projects or expansion due to restructuring.

How About Executive Search Firms? Can They Help?

That depends on what level you have reached in your career. Unless you can qualify for a job that pays over $50,000 a year, most search firms will not be interested in you.

Understand that search firms find people for jobs, *not* jobs for people. That is a profound difference. Search firms do not work for you; they work for their client companies.

In fact, many search firms (as well as employment agencies) are becoming quite specialized in the industries or functions they serve. We see firms searching *only* for financial managers, or sales managers, or managers in very specific industry fields such as entertainment, high tech, or energy. As the information age grows and expands through the 1990s and into the year 2000, this trend toward specialization will continue. Today, it is almost impossible for any search firm manager to stay abreast of changes and new developments in more than a single field. This trend means that the job seeker soliciting search firms must be aware of their specializations in order to minimize wasted time, money, and energy.

How Do Search Firms Get Paid?

A search firm is paid by an employer to find superior candidates for a particular job opening. The fee generally amounts to between twenty-five percent and thirty-five percent of the annual salary paid for the job. In other words, if the position pays $100,000 a year, the search firm stands to be paid a fee of between $25,000 and $35,000.

Actually, there are two types of search firms: retainer and contingency. The retainer firm enters into an exclusive arrangement with an employer to fill a particular opening. The firm is paid a percentage of the fee up front (before the search begins) and the remainder over the period of the search. A contingency firm is paid *only* if a candidate they have located is actually hired for the job. Theirs are nonexclusive arrangements, and it is common for a number of different contingency firms to be searching for candidates to fill the same job opening. Incidentally, contingency firms will occasionally handle positions that pay less than $50,000 a year, so if you are making less than this, it is a good idea to find out whether a firm is exclusively retained or contingency, because the former will not be interested in you but the latter may be.

Do you respond to and take notice of unsolicited letters and resumes?

"Yes. The most unlikely source may be a very valuable one."
  • **Russ Ringl, Corporate Director, Human Resources, American Medical Transport, Inc.**

How Do I Locate and Get in Touch with an Executive Search Firm?

First, try your local yellow pages. Search firms are usually listed under "executive search consultants" or sometimes under "management consultants" (but with these, phone before sending a resume— they may do other kinds of consulting, not executive searches). For a nationwide directory of executive search firms, refer to the *Directory of Executive Recruiters,* published by Kennedy & Kennedy. Your local library may have a copy, but if not you can order a copy (for approximately $31.00) by writing to: Kennedy & Kennedy, Templeton Road, Fitzwilliam, NH 03447.

Once you have identified a search firm, try and arrange an interview or meeting through a personal contact, someone who knows someone in the firm. If that fails, write a letter briefly outlining your experience and the type of position in which you are interested. Include a resume, and be sure to indicate the salary range that you need. Then follow up your letter with a telephone call a few days later. Be realistic about your chances, however. Many search firms receive hundreds of resumes each week. Only a very small percentage, perhaps as little as two to four percent, actually qualify for a position that the firm is attempting to fill at the time. And time is money to these people, so don't expect much attention.

Again, your chances for consideration will improve if you can somehow arrange a face-to-face meeting. You never know what assignments will come in next week or next month, and having seen you in person, the search executive is more likely to remember you.

Are Search Firms Really Worth the Bother?

Sure. Just don't pin all your hopes on finding a job through one of them. If you meet the standards necessary to qualify for consideration by search firms, you have nothing to lose by contacting as many as possible. Our advice is to send a letter and resume, then call and try to arrange a meeting. If you can't arrange a meeting forget that firm; they will call you if you fit a search they are conducting.

However, here is some good advice. Before you send your resume to a search firm, phone to see who is in charge of your specialty, your functional area. Tell that person's secretary that you will be sending a resume. That way, you will be writing to a partner or senior manager, rather than letting a lower-level researcher decide whether you are kept or "trashed."

If a Search Firm Calls Me, How Should I Respond? What Do I Tell Them?

Assuming you have gotten a message and are to call them back, be sure to place the call from a quiet, private place. If they are calling you, and if you have no office door to shut, call them back at a better time—that is never a problem. Next, be honest. Don't be coy or secretive, or try to "expand" your degrees, experience, responsibility, or titles. These folks have ways of trapping you, and if you haven't been straight, they will drop you like a hot potato. You'd better be honest about your salary too. Also, don't expect free advice or an overly long conversation. Answer the recruiter's questions quickly, but with an eye to the problems you have solved and the *real* responsibilities you have had.

Ask if the recruiter has an assignment, and probe as to what it is and how you might fit. Even if the job is way off base, try to meet with the head-hunter. After all, even though the current search may not fit you, tomorrow is another day, and maybe there will be a search that *will* fit. And, a personal meeting always puts you a step ahead, because now the head-hunter has you in the computer. Also remember that legitimate executive recruiters are *always* paid by the *employer*. If a recruiter asks you for money, such as a registration fee, hang up!

Then too, there are a lot of "one-man-bands" in the search business. Some of these folks work out of their homes and/or phone booths. This doesn't mean they are not competent; it simply means they are small. Therefore, don't expect them to have a long list of clients, and don't spend a long time or pin a lot of hopes on one of them. Going in to see their offices can usually give you an idea about the size of a recruiting firm.

Once I Have Been Called by a Search Firm, How Soon Will I Know If I Am a Candidate for a Job?

That depends on a lot of factors. For example, you may be eliminated for various reasons after your initial conversation, or you may end up a finalist among a selected few being considered for the position. The time frame is somewhat controlled by how long the search has been active at the time you are called. If contact is made at the beginning of the search (a search may take between two and six months to complete), the recruiter and employer may not be anxious to narrow the field until more candidates have been uncovered. On the other hand, if you are called midway into the search, or after they have been working on it for a considerable length of time, you can expect some pretty quick action. When you are called, simply ask the recruiter how long he or she has been working on the search.

Sometimes a problem can occur when the final three to five candidates are presented to the client company, but the client can't make up its mind. In this case, two things can happen: either more time is needed for interviewing the finalists, or none are chosen (which may mean the search goes back to square one). In a nutshell, you never know how long the process will take.

If I Send My Resume to One Office of a National Search Firm or Employment Agency, Will It Be on Their Computer for Other Offices?

Maybe, but don't count on it. Search firms get such huge volumes of resumes each week that they only computerize a small percentage of them. So play it safe, and send your resume to the search firm office in each city you are considering, just to be sure.

What was the most unusual ad response you have ever received? Was it effective?

"A letter stating they were a quality candidate and would submit a resume for $100. Not effective."
  • Joe Wegener, Vice President/Personnel, A.P.I. Alarm Systems

---

What About Employment Agencies? Should I Consider Them?

Employment agencies do deserve consideration. They usually specialize in jobs from entry level to perhaps $45,000 or $50,000 a year. These agencies make their fees through quick turnover, so it's likely that if they send you on an interview, they are also sending many others as well.

You will be asked to sign an application. Be sure to read it carefully before signing. Although most *employers* now pick up the agency fee, you could be signing a document that amounts to a contract, obligating *you* to pay the agency a percentage of your new salary.

Are There Any Other Published Sources for Jobs?

Sure. For example, depending upon your career field, some trade journals carry employment ads, and even trade associations can be helpful. The *Wall Street Journal* and the *National Business Employment Weekly* (published by the *Journal*) feature hundreds of job opportunities available throughout the country as well as overseas. For the most part, these are professional and managerial-level vacancies.

"Let me assure you, Winslow—there is no place for ego in this organization."

Don't forget that your state Employment Development or Personnel Department (state job development departments can be given a variety of names) can provide solid leads for both government and non-government jobs. And of course there is always the federal government's Civil Service Commission, representing thousands of job categories. Also, you can CREATE a job for yourself in government too—just research their problems and get to the hiring person that has them.

Now, a final reminder. While the published job market should not be overlooked, it is critical that you understand its limitations. Never—we repeat—*never*, depend on finding a job through these sources alone. If you do, you will significantly reduce your chances of finding the *right* job. At best, the published job market should be a supplement to your other, more productive efforts: your networking and direct contacts.

Strategies for the 90s

Back to School?

"A gap is growing between the skills possessed by our current and future work force, making education and training an issue."
  • Ann McLaughlin, former U.S. Secretary of Labor, discussing statistics from "Project 2000" by the Bureau of Labor Statistics and "Workforce 2000," a study commissioned by the Labor Department, as quoted in the *Los Angeles Times*, 4/2/89

For a B.A.—absolutely! No matter what. In the nineties, as the baby boom generation and its great numbers of people, reaches middle and senior management, the competition is going to be fierce. The B.A. degree is going to be nearly mandatory for any management position. If nothing else, it is a sign of acceptability, indicating that you are an "okay person" socially and professionally. The B.A. at least allows doors to open, even for those long past college age.

In addition, definitely plan to go back for as much training in specific functional or technical areas as you can. These specialized courses are usually of short duration and probably won't be a burden on your time or budget. This kind of periodic re-training can keep you up-to-date on your specialty and can broaden your understanding of business in general.

For advanced degrees, however, the further you get from college age, the less is the real need for them in non-technical fields. These degrees are very, very helpful in the first few years of working (they give you a "leg-up" on those who don't have them) and they always will be, all things being equal. But all things are seldom equal, and the older one becomes, the more emphasis is placed on, "What have you done lately and what can you do for me now?" (i.e., "How will *your* immediate past help me with *my* immediate present?")

So, what we are saying is that if the company pays for the advanced degree, terrific—go! But, if the cost of the degree is on you, think about it. It is two to six years of toil and time away from your family, as well as considerable out-of-pocket costs that may affect your family both physically and emotionally. The M.B.A., for instance, could cost you an enormous amount and might not even result in more money or a better job after you get the degree, depending on your age and level in the organization. Instead, consider planning your career in better ways. Do a better job of planning your work and working your plan.

To compete in the coming decade, a young man or woman should acquire:

"excellent communication skills. To compete, a candidate must be able to write extremely well, express him/herself well and direct the communication to the audience. In an interview, a candidate must be articulate and comfortable in the communication process."

> • Barbara Mitchell, Director of Human Resources, Host International

---

What changes do you foresee in the decade ahead?

"Fewer middle management jobs. Wider span of control. Need for computer literacy. More emphasis on pay for *real* results, not for just showing up."

> • M. Jennings, Senior Vice President/Personnel, Gannett Company

Strategies for the 90s

Staff vs. Line

In the nineties, try to stay away from too many staff positions. In staff positions, accomplishments tend to be team-oriented, and it is sometimes tough for any one person to really claim total responsibility for a particular stellar result. Also, in a staff position, you probably will not have profit and loss responsibility, something you *must* have if you are going to make it to senior management.

Line positions frequently show off your potential much better than staff positions (in a company as well as in a resume), and it is here that one is frequently given profit and loss responsibility. So plan ahead for line assignments such as regional manager, sales manager (or v.p.), or production manager (or v.p.) rather than staff positions like controller, assistant to the president, or personnel director.

In the decade ahead, we will see:

"greater segmentation of the job market. Competition for qualified technical graduates will get stronger given the declining enrollments in science and engineering disciplines. These graduates will be in high demand, and starting salaries will rise accordingly.

Requirements for office and operating jobs will get more stringent because of higher technical content on the jobs. Although there will be many candidates for each job opening, the proportion of *qualified* candidates will decrease. The skills gap will continue to increase. Competition for qualified candidates will increase."

- Chris Lardge, Manager, Employment,
  Chevron Corporation

WHAT'S OUT THERE—
RESEARCHING THE JOB MARKET

How important is research? Place it at the top of your list. Broadly speaking, just about every aspect of your job search is fueled by research, from targeting potential employers, to preparing for that all-important interview, to making your final decision about a job offer. Without adequate and reliable information, the mental tug of war that leads you to a proper decision can just as easily lead you into faulty judgment and a costly mistake.

In some instances, research is the only way to get started. Many of us spend years in what might be called comfortable isolation, oblivious to all outside activity that is not of immediate personal concern. It is only after we are compelled to look for a new job that the notion strikes us—often with the force of a jackhammer—that we are not really prepared for the task at hand. Our knowledge of other companies in the field turns out to be surprisingly limited. The only way to get up to speed quickly is through research. It is an important way to find companies with job opportunities.

Finding the right job also means finding the right employer. Short of your being desperate, it makes little sense to pursue a company whose manner of doing business is significantly at odds with your own belief system. For the marriage to succeed, one of you will have to alter your way of thinking, and it is a pretty safe bet it will not be your employer. So, why invite conflict and hardship by going into a job blindly? If you have done a thorough job of researching a prospective employer in advance of being offered a job, your decision will become that much easier, and, if you choose to accept the offer, the potential for disappointment and surprises will be held to a minimum.

The gathering of information is a key ingredient in any successful job-search campaign. It can open the door to opportunity and protect you from errors in judgment. While much of your research is informal, indeed almost daily ritual (like glancing through the want ads and speaking with friends and associates), it is the time-consuming task of formalized research that will ultimately pay the highest dividend. It is important that you take this aspect of the job search very seriously. Good research is priceless, and failing to do enough research may cost you some golden opportunities.

How can a candidate maximize his or her chances of being hired?

"Research the company, the manager, the HR person (or interviewer), the competition, etc."
> • Russ Ringl, Corporate Director, Human Resources,
> American Medical Transport, Inc.

How thorough a knowledge of your company do you expect a candidate to have?

"A high degree. It is very important for the candidate to have done extensive research *and* be prepared to ask questions based on that research. This applies to entry level as well as senior managers although the amount and depth might vary."
> • Barbara Mitchell, Director of Human Resources,
> Host International

How Do I Begin My Research?

Chances are you have already begun, assuming you have a number of target companies in mind. If not, your first assignment is to compile a list of potential employers. At this point, try not to be judgmental. Think about and write down the names of as many companies as you can that might need someone with your particular skills and experience. If you run out of names, check out a trade directory for your industry or kind of business and talk to friends and associates, they may come up with some possible employers you haven't thought about.

What If I End Up with Dozens of Companies on My List?

Nothing wrong with that. The broader the field, the better your chances of finding the right job. But, at the moment, you are concerned with research—comprehensive research—so it will be far too time-consuming to attempt to thoroughly investigate each and every company on your list. Once your list is complete, you will have to narrow it down to ten or twelve prime targets.

How Do I Narrow Down My List without Researching Each Company?

That is a tough question, with no easy answer. At this stage, you simply have to make some judgment calls. Utilize your experience, knowledge of the field, even intuition. Apply some personal qualifiers that are easy to identify, such as location, size, reputation, etc. Talk to your network of contacts—friends and associates. One or more may have solid knowledge of many of the companies on your list. Better yet, someone in your network may have a personal friend in one of the companies, perhaps even a decision-maker. Once you have decided on your prime targets, do not discard the others. They can become secondary targets for your broadcast letters, which we will discuss in our chapter on self-marketing and creating buyer interest. Some of these secondary companies may even become prime targets later in your job search.

Okay, So Now I Have Ten or Twelve Prime Targets. What's Next?

Now, the work really begins. You have selected a number of companies that you think look interesting. Okay, how do you convince them that they need you? A major step in that process is to prepare for your first contact and/or interview by learning as much about the company as you possibly can—its history, product or service line, financial condition, competition, corporate culture, ethical standards, size, operating procedure, and so on. And for your trouble, you will receive double value!

We have already established that your goal is not simply to find a job but to find the *right* job. To do that, you must evtually make an informed and intelligent decision about accepting an offer. To a large extent, the correctness of that decision will depend on how well you have done your homework, how thoroughly you have researched the company making you an offer. Does the company meet *your* needs? That is a question that should be first and foremost in your mind.

How thorough a knowledge of your company do you expect a candidate to have when he or she arrives for an interview?

"Good working knowledge. They should at least know and understand product line, sales, and profit history."
  • **R. B. Hennessy, Vice President/Human Resources, National Starch & Chemical**

Where Can I Find All This Research Information?

A good starting point is your local public or university library. Get to know the reference librarian. He or she can be very helpful in directing your research. At the end of this chapter, you will find an extensive list of business publications and directories that are available at most reasonably sized libraries. They can provide much of the information you will need.

You'll also want to talk with friends and associates familiar with the company or companies you are researching. If you can make contact with an employee—It doesn't have to be a decision-maker—who will join you for lunch or even a brief meeting, you can come away with valuable inside information about company culture and employee satisfaction. You may even learn something about the problems currently facing the company. Though it takes a bit of courage, we have actually had some clients who have stopped employees in the company parking lot to talk with them.

Besides the business publications, you will also find indexes that can lead you to articles about the company you are researching. Most large libraries retain, either in original form or on microfilm, copies of these publications. Recent articles are always a good source of information because they generally reflect the current condition of the company or some unusual aspect that is worth noting.

Also, if the company you are researching is publicly held, get a copy of its annual report and "10K." Generally, you can get these reports by contacting the company directly, usually the treasurer's office. They can reveal a lot of valuable information about financial condition, company mission, company philosophy of doing business, product or service line, as well as the names of the men and women who run the organization. You can also get a feel for whether the company is in a growth phase or has already matured and is threatened with eventual decline. The president's message to stockholders (usually on the first page or so of the annual report) will tell you what the company failed to do in the past year (in other words, problems that need solving), as well as what management wants to do in the coming year (in other words, opportunities for the future).

One caution. Although most of the business directories you will use are current, they cannot possibly be completely up-to-date. Names and titles change frequently. Don't assume that this critical information is accurate. Before you try to contact an individual listed in a directory, be sure to phone the company to confirm that the person still holds the same position. While you are at it, double-check the spelling of their name and title.

How thorough a knowledge of your company do you expect a candidate to have?

"Unless they are absolutely stunning, I expect them to know as much about the company as I do. That means they have *at least* read the annual report."

> • Doug Cooper, Vice President/Personnel,
> Valero Energy Corporation

"I'd like a book that ranks companies according to perks."

What If I Discover that a Company I Am Researching Isn't All that I Expected It To Be?

If its problems are truly significant and fundamental, drop the company from your list of prime targets and replace it with another. Remember, you are looking for the *right* job, not just any job. That means you have to be comfortable with your job and the company.

Through research, you will learn information about each of your target companies that can help you decide on how to approach them. You will need to determine if your skills and interests make a good match with the company's needs, as well as how to highlight your skills and experience, even if you are going after a job that has not yet been publicly announced or perhaps doesn't yet exist. Yes, that's right! That's what your research can uncover.

The very clever actions of a former client of ours illustrates this point. This fellow was a vice president of sales, but had set a CEO job as his next career move. His unique strategy was to research and talk to banks and investment banking firms in the area, in order to find small to mid-sized companies in trouble. He was led to one whose principal problem was sales (or lack of sales, to be exact). The company couldn't afford both a high-priced v.p. of sales and a high-priced president. So the company's board of directors hired our client as the new president, but with a second hat to wear, that of sales director. Here, then, was a job that was unlisted, unpublished, and just waiting to be defined and landed by a guy who did his research in a creative way.

Now, even though you may not be in a vice-presidential slot, you can see the value of matching up your goals and research for your next career move, as our client did. Research will show you where the company is, the names of the players, and the problems the company is facing, ones that you may be able to help them solve. You can then strategize, based on your goals, to gain the most from situations you uncover at any level in the organization.

How thorough a knowledge of your company do you expect a candidate to have when he or whe arrives for an interview?

"[I expect candidates to know about our] products, our competitors, our sales volume, and our location."
• Joe Wegener, Vice President/Personnel, A.P.I. Alarm Systems

"I expect a candidate to have little specific knowledge since we are privately held. However, an impressive candidate is one who has gone to one of our stores and can conceptually articulate his/her impressions of who we are and what we stand for."
• Olon P. Zager, Director of Human Resources, Gucci

"Sure, they're an equal opportunity employer. They pay *everyone* minimum wage."

The importance of solid research simply cannot be over-emphasized. Your knowledge of the history and internal workings of an organization can provide an edge when you are competing with others for the same job. When you are researching a company, think of yourself as a detective looking for clues to an angle that may get you through the door. Look for problems that you can solve or areas in which your skills can fill a void. The thoroughness of your research will be instantly communicated when you talk with company managers, so don't look for short cuts. The time you spend researching your target companies is, indeed, time very well spent.

Here is a sample index card that will help you organize your research.

Front

INC International

1133 Sarento Road

Contact: Joe Minor, Sales Manager, tel. 243–8692

Date Contacted	Method	Date of reply	Results
1. Sept. 9	Telephone call		Interview
2. Sept. 12	Personal interview		Referral
3. Sept. 15	Personal interview		Resume requested
4. Sept. 16	Resume sent 9/20		Call from dept. head
5. Sept. 23	Interview		Job offer

Back

Pertinent Information about This Organization and Specific Department

Sales department seems to be disorganized. Needs market research to identify target market for new product line to be introduced in six months. Sales down thirty percent from last year.

How To Use Industry Reference Books

In the business reference section of the library:

1. Look up the industry in the alphabetical section and discover appropriate SIC code.
2. Then, in SIC section, decide on target companies.
3. Research backgrounds of individual executives and other pertinent data.
4. Analyze annual reports and other, more detailed corporate materials.

If you have problems, ask the business librarian for help.

The SIC Numbers: A Valuable Key in Your Market Research

The Standard Industrial Classification (SIC) was developed for use in the classification of establishments by the type of activity in which they are engaged. These ten classifications are intended to cover the entire field of economic activities in:

Agriculture, forestry, fishing, hunting, and trapping
Mining
Construction
Manufacturing
Transportation, communication, electric, gas, and sanitary services
Wholesale trade
Retail trade
Finance, insurance, and real estate
Personal services, business services, repair services, and other services
Public administration

The structure of the classification makes it possible to tabulate, analyze, and publish this data in a way that is very helpful in a job search with target companies. The following is a selection of research directories that can be found in most medium to large public libraries. We do not suggest that our list is complete, as there are many dozens of business-related books and directories available. If you can clearly describe your specific needs, a research librarian can easily lead you to the best source for that information.

American Electronics Association Directory
American Electronics Association, 2600 El Camino Rd., Palo Alto, CA 94306

> Annual alphabetical listing of member electronics companies, including names of officers and marketed products.

Business Directory, Chamber of Commerce

> Includes major employers, Chamber member businesses and their presidents or managers, as well as products and services. Available through local Chambers of Commerce.

Dictionary of Occupational Titles
U.S. Department of Labor, Government Printing Office, Washington D.C. 20212

> Code numbers and descriptions of 20,000 job titles, covering nearly all jobs in the U.S. economy.

Directory of Corporate Affiliations (Who Owns Whom)
National Register Publishing Co., Inc., 3004 Glenview Rd., Wilmette, Ill 60091

> Gives a view of the corporate structure of more than 4,000 major U.S. companies and their 40,000 subsidiaries, divisions, and affiliates.

Directory of Executive Recruiters
Consultants News, Templeton Road, Fitzwilliam, N.H. 03447

> A listing of over 2,000 executive recruiters nationwide, including the names of key principals at each firm and hints on how to work with recruiters. Updated annually.

Dun's Guide to Healthcare Companies
Dun's Marketing Services, Inc., Three Century Drive, Parsippany, NJ
07054

Hard-to-find data on 15,000 healthcare manufacturers and suppliers. Includes a key word index in professional and layman's
terms.

Dun's Career Guide
Dun's Marketing Services, Inc., Three Century Drive, Parsippany, NJ
07054

Describes career opportunities and hiring practices of more than
5,000 companies.

Electronics Marketing Directory
Dun's Marketing Services, Inc., Three Century Drive, Parsippany, NJ
07054

A useful guide to the multibillion dollar electronics industry. Lists
8000 manufacturers within specific product categories.

Encyclopedia of Associations
Gale Research Company, Book Tower, Detroit, Michigan 48226

Comprehensive list of national associations, including names of
chief officers. statement of activities, number of members and
names of publications. Three volumes.

Macmillan Directory of Leading Private Companies
National Register Publishing Co. Inc., 3004 Glenview Rd., Wilmette,
IL 60091

Provides comprehensive data on approximately 9,500 parent
companies and wholly-owned subsidiaries in the United States.
Listings are arranged alphabetically, detailing the following information: company name, address, telephone/telex numbers, SIC
codes and a description of the company's business and products.

Million Dollar Directory Series
Dun's Marketing Services, Inc., Three Century Drive, Parsippany, NJ
07054

Provides detailed information on more than 160,000 of America's
largest companies—both public and private. Includes key facts on
decision-makers, company size and line of business. Five volumes.

Moody's Industrial Manual
Moody's Investors Services, Inc., 99 Church St., New York, New
York 10007

Classification by industry and product. History of companies, including their operations, subsidiaries, plants, products, key executives, comparative income statements, balance sheets, and
outstanding securities. Two volumes.

Occupational Outlook Handbook
U.S. Bureau of Labor Statistics, Government Printing Office, Washington, D.C. 20212

This handbook describes several hundred occupations and includes information on necessary training, employment prospects,
earnings, and working conditions. Revised every two years.

Small Business Bibliographies
Small Business Administration, 1441 L. St., Washington, D.C. 20416

A broad listing of trade journals and government and nongovern-
ment publications, covering a wide variety of business activities.

Standard & Poor's Register of Corporations, Directors and Executives
Standard & Poor's Corporation, 25 Broadway, New York, New York
10004

Alphabetical listing of over 50,000 corporations including zip
codes, telephone numbers, names, titles, and functions of approx-

imately 450,000 officers, directors, and other principals. Also includes description of company's product/services and, where available, annual sales and number of employees. Three volumes.

Standard Directory of Advertising Agencies (Agency Red Book)
National Register Publishing Co., Inc., 3004 Glenview Rd., Wilmette, IL 60091

This volume lists 4,000 advertising agencies, 27,000 personnel by title, and 60,000 accounts. Issued three times a year.

Reference Book of Corporate Managements
Dun's Marketing Services, Inc., Three Century Drive, Parsippany, NJ 07054

Biographical profiles of principal officers and directors in more than 12,000 leading U.S. companies. Four volumes.

Sample Research Fact Sheet

Company: O.C. Tanner

Overview: O.C. Tanner designs and produces comprehensive employee recognition programs. This service includes creative design of awards, promotional materials, guidelines for presentations, and program administration. The awards include high quality, custom-designed emblems of gold and precious stones placed on jewelry accessories, custom-designed rings, medallions, and plaques, as well as a variety of commemorative gifts. These awards are given to employees for service, safety, sales, productivity, and other achievements.

Clientele:
- Tanner serves sixty percent of the Fortune 1000 Companies with recognition programs.
- Over 13,000 corporations have bought recognition programs from O.C. Tanner.
- Tanner desi ns recognition programs for more of the Fortune 1000 companies than its four closest competitors combined.

Mobil	RCA	Bank of America
Shell Oil	Woolworth	Conoco
Chrysler	Firestone Tire	American Stock Exchange
Dow Chemical	& Rubber	The Royal Bank of Canada
Eastman Kodak	PepsiCo	Simpsons-Sears, Ltd.
Standard Oil	Getty Oil	Canadian Superior Oil, Ltd.
(Ohio)	Blue Bell	Burlington

Company Profile:
- O.C. Tanner is the largest U.S. manufacturer of corporate emblematic jewelry.
- Privately held.
- Average annual sales growth over the past ten years has been about twenty percent.
- 1,200 employees are located at the corporate office and factory in Salt Lake City, Utah.
- O.C. Tanner is represented by sales people in all fifty states and Canada.

Production:
- Over two million awards are produced yearly.
- Each emblem takes over forty hand-operations to produce.

Origins: The company was founded in 1927 by Obert C. Tanner, philosophy professor, who taught at the University of Utah and

Stanford University. His company was originally set up in the basement of his mother's home in Salt Lake City to produce seminary pins for students completing the Bible study class. A well-known business and community leader, Obert Tanner has made significant philanthropic contributions to education and the arts.

Attached Magazine/Newspaper Articles

Research Fact Sheet

Company:

Overview:

Clientele:

Company Profile:

Production:

Origins:

Attached Magazine/Newspaper Articles

Strategies for the 90s

"**Instant performance** will be expected of [tomorrow's managers], and it's going to be harder to hide incompetence."
- Ann Barry, Vice President/Research, Handy Associates, Inc., a New York consulting firm, as quoted in Carol Hymowitz, "Day in the Life of Tomorrow's Manager," *Wall Street Journal*, March 20, 1989.

One's age is always a factor in the job market, and it will continue to be a factor in the 1990s. Obviously, a twenty-five-year-old is not likely to be chosen as a CEO of a Fortune 500 company; at twenty-five, a person has not yet left enough shoe leather on the street. On the other hand, a sixty-two-year-old probably is not going to be chosen for heavy construction work.

Aside from these kinds of obvious "non-fits," the real issue here is what the person can do to resolve situations or solve problems. There is age bias against all ages, depending upon who's talking, but the overriding factor is, "What can you do for me?" not "How old are you?"

Age bias is another reason to do your research and plan your attack. Know what needs to be done in a company, then overlay your talents and abilities onto those needs and problems. Show them why you are the best person for the job.

As a practical matter it should be noted that a trend is developing among many larger organizations—that of hiring fewer job applicants in their fifties and sixties for full-time employment. Thus, rather than trying to enter into only these larger companies, we suggest that an older job seeker also consider smaller organizations that may not be considered the elite or a leader in an industry. In these smaller environments, competition for jobs from younger "hot shot" candidates may not be as intense. An older worker might also consider becoming a consultant (not a full-time employee), thus selling his or her expertise gained over many years. This career transition may require some training as to how to establish a consulting business, but many such courses can be found in local colleges and universities, as well as through social service agencies for senior citizens.

Also don't forget about buying or working in a franchise business. Many such opportunities can be found in local small business expos and/or in newspaper and industry periodicals.

Yes, age is an important consideration in career planning, but there's a place for everyone. Just look around you, be aware of opportunities and your abilities, and be realistic.

Do you have any advice for female, minority, or older candidates?

"**Sell the employer** on your professional skills without regard to your age, sex, or minority status."
  • Thomas J. Haines, Corporate Director, Human Resources, Fairchild Industries, Inc.

Strategies for the 90s

Job Hopping

"**We will soon find ourselves** cycling in and out of several different careers throughout our lives, each interspersed with periods of rest, recreation, retraining and personal reflection."
  • Ken Dychtwald and Joe Flower, *Age Wave*

Job hopping is no longer the problem it once was, but only do it for good reasons, and don't do it without a master plan. Take charge of your career! Don't job hop unless a new job gives you several advantages.

  • A chance to leapfrog on your long-term plan.
  • More responsibility in your current function.

"No, no, Mr. Winslow! I said a relationship with a company was *like* a marriage!"

• A broader scope of cross-functional knowledge and experience.
• A minimum twenty-five percent increase in salary *and* benefits or perks.

A lateral move in a new company with only a twenty-five percent increase should be looked at very carefully. The learning curve and downtime needed for adapting to the new firm's corporate culture, politics, and products or services can be big time-wasters for your career, unless there are clear and viable career reasons for the move.

How do you feel about candidates with a history of
job hopping?

"**Job hoppers are like** overqualified candidates. I will take all I
can get as long as they can do the job while they last."
> • Doug Cooper, Vice President/Personnel,
> Valero Energy Corporation

"**Job hopping is a particular concern** when it represents a
continuous pattern. Whether or not this is a problem for an
employer depends upon company objectives. The one thing that
is obvious is that someone who has a record of changing jobs
every two to five years will have a high probability of continuing
that pattern with the next employer."
> • James E. McElwain, Vice President/Personnel Resources,
> NCR Corporation

"**This depends on the position and age** of the applicant. I am
willing to risk hiring a job hopper for a hard-to-find skill."
> • Joe Wegener, Vice President/Personnel,
> A. P. I. Alarm System

CREATING BUYER INTEREST— SELF-MARKETING

A successful job search has much in common with the launching of a new consumer product. Both projects must pass through three similar stages. The first stage is the identification of a buyer (research). The next stage is the development of a strategy designed to reach that buyer (marketing). And then comes the payoff—making the sale.

Truth-in-advertising laws prohibit the use of false claims, so most advertisers go to great lengths, through words and images, to make their product appear to be the most appealing and desirable on the market. In a sense, you must do the same thing. A potential employer must be made to believe that you are the *best* candidate on the market and that if they fail to offer you a position with the company, they will lose a valuable asset.

Like it or not, your combined skills, experience, talent, and personality add up to a single, unique "product." Through research, you have already identified your "buyer," the companies targeted as potential employers. Now it is time to create buyer interest and awareness through self-marketing. In every instance, your goal should be to arrange a face-to-face meeting, even if contact is being made purely for informational purposes. Your tools for arranging that all-important in-person meeting will be the telephone and the printed word, singularly and in combination. By mastering these two means of communication, you will have improved your chances tenfold of finding and winning the right job.

If I Want To Contact a Potential Employer, Should I Write or Telephone?

Pick up the phone and place a call. The telephone should always be your *first* choice. Then you can, and should, follow up your conversation with a letter.

Why Is It Better To Phone Than To Write?

For a number of reasons, not the least of which is the efficient use of your time. You can place a call and speak with a decision-maker faster than you can write a letter, let alone put it in the mail and wait for a response. Another strong reason for favoring the telephone is flexibility. By hearing a voice at the other end, you can quickly assess the response you are receiving and adjust accordingly. The telephone provides a more personal approach as well. It allows you to take full advantage of your personality and persuasive abilities.

There are, of course, times when a letter is necessary and even more appropriate. If you are simply unable to reach your target by phone (and some of these people can be very slippery), or you want to cover a large number of low-priority potential employers—perhaps at distant locations—then turn to your self-marketing letter.

I'm Not Very Good on the Telephone. I Get Nervous and Panic Easily, Especially When I'm Calling a Stranger. What Can I Do about It?

An old joke poses the question, "How do I get to Carnegie Hall?" The answer to that joke is the best advice we can offer: "Practice, practice, practice!"

If that sounds simplistic, it is not meant to be. Nothing builds confidence better than continued practice and knowing that you are fully prepared for the task. If you have done a thorough job of researching the company, and you have rehearsed what you are going to say—and that includes anticipating what might be said or asked of you in response to your call—then you have little to fear.

Certainly, you are bound to meet with some rejection—it can't be helped—but it is important that you maintain perspective. In most cases, it is not *you* being rejected, but your telephone call, and the rejection is the result of factors over which you have little control such as timing, the busy schedule of the party you are trying to reach, or even that person's personality (which may include a tendency not to be easily cornered). Remember, your call, especially to those who don't know you, is not a high priority, so don't let it get you down. Hang in there and be persistent.

All of the above notwithstanding, a fear of the telephone is a common affliction. Its root cause lies in a change of roles. Ordinarily, you would be using the telephone to speak with friends, answer questions, assist others, or to be placing business calls with the security of an established company behind you. Now, however, you are asking others for help, representing only yourself, without the security and confidence of a title or employer to validate your call. It is not a situation to which you are accustomed.

In many instances, however, it is perfectly all right to use the name of your former employer as an introductory reference: "This is John Doe of Consolidated Industries . . ." Such an approach can be helpful in getting you through to the person you are calling, and even if you have been laid off (temporarily or permanently) it is highly unlikely that your former employer will object, especially if it helps you find new employment.

Another fear is the anticipation that a verbal mistake can be fatal, that you won't be able to recover as quickly, or as convincingly, on the phone as you would in a face-to-face meeting. However, if you have done your homework, a serious error is highly unlikely, so let's add another admonition: Prepare, prepare, prepare!

How Should I Rehearse These Calls?

The best way is with a tape recorder. Practice your introduction again and again, until it becomes second nature. Listen to the recordings with a critical ear. Do you sound forthright and sincere? Are you stating the purpose of your call clearly and succinctly? Ask a trusted friend or family member to critique your introduction.

Now here are some other points you will want to remember when preparing for and making your self-marketing calls:

1. Always phone from a quiet place, one that is free of distractions.
2. Never lose sight of your objective. You are going after an interview, not a job.
3. Be absolutely certain that you have the name of the right person to be contacted.
4. Have a strategy and tactic in mind before making the call. Create a check list of points you want to cover, and keep that check list close at hand when you phone.
5. Try to anticipate the possible responses you may receive. Above all, be prepared with an answer to the most common question you are likely to hear: "Why are you calling?" It is amazing how many people stumble over this most obvious and elementary question.
6. Be prepared to discuss your accomplishments and what you feel you have to offer. Even if you are phoning to follow up on a referral or letter of introduction, don't expect the party you are calling to remember who you are. Play it safe, and assume that he or she does not remember you.
7. Be direct. Come to the point as quickly and as clearly as possible.
8. Be as brief as possible. Once you have accomplished the purpose of your call, hang up—don't meander or draw out the conversation.
9. Speak with sincerity and a strong voice. A weak voice and hesitant manner will immediately send out a negative signal.

How Do I Handle a Difficult Secretary?

With kid gloves. Or at least with respect and patience. Remember, in most cases, a secretary is only doing his or her job, carrying out specific screening instructions. If you are forced to phone a number of times, try to develop a friendly relationship with this person. If you have handled the situation properly, a secretary can be very helpful in gaining access to the person you are trying to reach.

If I Am Having Trouble Getting Through, How Many Times Should I Call Back?

As often as you like, within reason. If the person whom you are calling is out, leave your name only; then try to find out the best time to call again. If you obtain that information, be sure to phone again at the suggested time. The repeated appearance of your name on your target person's desk will arouse curiosity and will eventually lead to the acceptance of a call.

How Hard Should I Push for an Interview?

That is something you have to judge for yourself. If the resistance is *really* strong, back off and try another tack; you still have an opportunity to produce favorable results. Remember, the object of each call is to get the person you are phoning to do something that will help your job-search campaign. Ask about other potential employers or other decision-makers within the company. If the person offers any suggestions, ask permission to use his or her name as a referral. Even if there are no openings at present, suggest a date you could call back for an interview in anticipation of future openings.

Regardless of the outcome of each phone conversation, be sure to follow up with a brief thank-you note.

Is There a Best Time To Make These Calls?

Morning seems to work best for most people. It is a new day; you are fresh from a good night's sleep, and the people you are trying to reach are not yet too deeply involved in their daily routine.

Plan to make a definite number of calls each and every working day. If you have trouble getting started, phone a friend first to warm up or to rehearse your introduction. If your goal is eight calls a day, don't quit until you have reached that number.

Think of your daily calls as a market-research study. You have something of value to sell, and what you are trying to do by phone is to quickly and efficiently identify serious buyers.

Although the telephone can at times be an intimidating instrument, it can also become your best friend and the most powerful and immediate tool you have at your disposal. Try hard to overcome any negative feelings you may have about its use. Like any other device, the more you use it, the more comfortable and secure you will become, and the more likely it is that you will discover a job opportunity that would otherwise have remained hidden.

What about Self-Marketing Letters?

The telephone may be the fastest way to reach a decision-maker, but, as we pointed out earlier, there are times when the self-marketing letter takes center stage. Your ability to write a good self-marketing letter and your use of these letters can have a powerful effect on your job search.

In actual fact, *any* letter you write in regard to your job-search campaign is a self-marketing letter. In every instance, even if it's only a brief thank-you note, you should be trying to convey a favorable impression. But a good impression is not enough. You want your letter to force the reader to take action—ideally, to invite you to call or stop by for a face-to-face interview.

The written word, when used effectively, can motivate, influence, and persuade. When used poorly, it cannot help but reveal deficiencies that the writer would otherwise prefer went unnoticed.

Basically, there are three types of self-marketing letters: the broadcast letter, the targeted letter, and the ad response letter. The content of these letters may be quite similar, but your approach to each will vary considerably.

What Is a Broadcast Letter?

"Broadcast letter" is a term commonly applied to a large mailing. Let's say that you have identified a large number of possible employers. They may be widely scattered or may represent, at best, long-shot chances for employment. A broadcast letter will announce your availability as quickly and as widely as possible, without your having to devote a great deal of time to research. In other words, you are throwing out a bunch of lines in hope that one of the fish may bite.

Do you respond to or take notice of unsolicited letters and resumes? Are they a good idea?

"All are read, evaluated, and lead to a response being generated. It costs money to obtain resumes either through ads or agencies. The unsolicited resumes arrive at zero cost and deserve full attention. Timing is important, but a number of key employees have joined the company because of unsolicited resumes."
> • C. E. Wild, Vice President/Human Resources, Ball Corporation

---

Are All Broadcast Letters the Same?

For the most part, they are. You may want to alter or target them by groups: letters going to advertising agencies, for instance, might be slightly different than those going to public relations firms. But the body of the letter can be pretty much the same.

How Many Broadcast Letters Should I Send Out?

It is not a matter of how many letters you send out overall—you may send out hundreds, if each company represents a legitimate employment possibility—but, rather, how many you send out at one time.

All job-search letters—even the broadcast letter—to be truly effective, must be followed up by a phone call, usually within ten days. Obviously, if you send out hundreds of broadcast letters in a single mailing, you will have trouble doing follow-up. Send out no more than ten or twelve a week. That way you will never be overwhelmed by the need for making hundreds of phone calls in a short period of time.

What About the Targeted Letter? How Does It Differ?

A target letter is a personalized or customized letter that goes to a company or individual that you have thoroughly researched but for one reason or another have been unable to reach by telephone. While the body of the letter may be quite similar to the broadcast letter, your opening should reflect the fact that you have done your homework and know a good deal about the company. In fact, if possible, you should lead off your letter by referring to a company need that you have identified. Catch the reader's attention by mentioning something that he or she *wants* to hear. Once you have hooked the reader, you can go on to tell your own story.

And the Ad Response Letter? Is It Different, Too?

Yes. But only in the sense that you have been given a clear indication of the job function, as well as the skills and experience necessary to fill the position. These insights should guide the writing of your letter.

The first thing to do is to isolate the key qualities that the advertiser seems to be looking for in a candidate. Then relate your own skills, talent, and experience to the needs of the advertiser. Work this blend into the first paragraph of your letter, copying the style and sequence of the ad.

If, for example, the ad begins something like this: "Needed: experienced copywriter with technical background," then, your opening paragraph should read something like this: "I am an experienced copywriter with a strong technical background."

The logic behind copying the content and sequence of an ad is this: most print ads, as we pointed out earlier, are little more than a lottery, with hundreds, perhaps even thousands, of responses expected. There will be two stacks—"yes" and "no." The person responsible for deciding which stack your letter goes into will be looking for any short cut possible to handle the volume of letters on his or her desk. Anytime there is an immediate match-up between company need and a candidate's response, it is almost certain that the letter will go straight into the "yes" stack, which, of course, is where you want to be. The rest of your letter should be brief, with an emphasis on your accomplishments.

Most unusual ad response:

"Candidate refused to drive five miles for the interview. She wanted us to come to her home as it would show that we had a genuine interest in her. After all, employment is a two-way street! This candidate was on a one-way street obviously going the *wrong* way!"
- Denny Wheeler, Manager, Corporate Human Resources, B. F. Goodrich

---

The most unusual ad response I've ever received was:

"The candidate wrote a hand written note with his resume saying, 'I'm experienced enough to do whatever you need in marketing. I hate looking for a job—it's hell! Hire me.' We did. He was quite successful."
- Vera Blanchet, Vice President/Human Resources, Corporate Headquarters, California Federal Savings & Loan Association

---

What was the most unusual ad response you've ever received? Was it effective?

"The unusual is likely not effective. I've seen it all: videos, cartoons, colored paper, 8" × 10" glossies, audio tapes, a talking resume."
- Gary Bernard, Senior Vice President/Human Resources, Dataproducts Corporation

---

Should I Include a Resume with These Letters?

We recommend that you do not include a resume. If you have written a good self-marketing letter, it will stand on its own. The reader will have learned enough about your background to decide whether or not to invite you in, and there is always the chance that by including your resume you will reveal some minor detail that might disqualify you before you get up to bat. Two exceptions to this rule would be regarding (1) a letter you are sending to an executive search firm, to whom you must always enclose a resume, and (2) a letter in response to a published ad in which the employer makes it clear that a resume is essential.

How Do I Know if I Have a Good Self-Marketing Letter?

That, of course, is a tough question. At the end of this chapter, you will find a number of examples of good self-marketing letters. We can't teach you to write effectively—that is an entire course in itself—but we can give you some guidelines.

The most important thing to keep in mind is that your opening paragraph *MUST* grab the reader's attention. You can do that in a variety of ways, but the most effective will always be by leading off with something that the reader wants to hear. That can only be determined by research.

Get to your point quickly, and don't overwrite. You are approaching busy people who don't have the time for, or an appreciation of, flowery prose. Their interest, by necessity, is in the bottom line. "What can this person do for me?," they ask. "And why should I go on with this letter?" Hook 'em early and you've got a chance!

Once you have the reader's interest and attention, you can tell your story in a more conventional way. But keep it brief and well-focused. Save your rambling letters for a friend or relative.

Always have your letters proofread several times before sending them out. Also make absolutely certain that you have not misspelled the recipient's name or gotten his or her title wrong. No matter how good your letters may be, it is all wasted effort if they include misspellings or typographical errors.

If you have any question about the effectiveness of your self-marketing letters, ask the opinion of others. A fresh perspective is always helpful.

And one final suggestion: always use the "five whats" of letter communication when writing to your network referrals, target companies, search firms, and so on. They are:

1. What happened (if you've been laid off).
2. What job you want.
3. What location you want.
4. What you want the person to do.
5. What day and time you will be contacting the person.

Samples of Self-Marketing Letters

Sample *Broadcast Letter:*

Name
Title
Company
Address

Dear _____:

For the past seven years I have been involved in providing Escrow services to the Real Estate industry. My background includes all aspects of the business from origination (sales) to title examination and insurance to document preparation and settlement. I have had total responsibility for an organization of 60 people, seven branches, and an operating budget of $4 million. I am exploring opportunities in which I can utilize my background and experience.

My accomplishments include:

- Expanded a single operation into seven branches covering three counties in less than four years.
- Increased revenue from $750,000 to $6,500,000, which resulted in a 28% increase in profits.
- Installed computerized programs for both accounting and document preparation which substantially reduced errors and increased employee productivity. This installation accounted for 8% of the increase in profits.
- Created a feeder network of attorneys and other merger and acquisition experts which provided an increase in title insurance income of 12%.

These represent only a few of my achievements. I will be happy to discuss my capabilities in greater detail, as related to your needs, in a personal interview. I will give you a call next week to arrange an interview.

Sincerely,

Sample *Broadcast Letter:*

Name
Title
Company
Address

Dear _____ :

As executive secretary to the vice president of syndication at Premier Studios, I have more than eight years of experience in office management, syndicated television sales/distribution, statistical reports, contracts, word processing, and general secretarial procedures.

My accomplishments include:

- Maintained reports and tracked sales on twelve first-run programs in nationwide distribution.
- Acted as liaison with executives and staff at all levels of television stations.
- Coordinated sales contract preparation from initial sale to final acceptance.

I am relocating to the New York area this year and am looking for a position that would provide me with an opportunity to expand my experience in the field of syndication. I am aware of your organization's fine reputation in the international market and would appreciate an opportunity to discuss my plans with you.

I will be in New York later this month, and I will call you to see if there is a convenient time that we might meet.

Sincerely,

Sample *Broadcast Letter:*

Name
Title
Company
Address

Dear _____:

I am an assistant vice president with five years experience in marketing "loan and deposit" services. Within the past calendar year, I have booked 10 million dollars in new loans, 1.5 million in demand deposits, and 3 million in certificates of deposit (180 day maturities).

My resaons for seeking new employment are two-fold: a desire to tackle greater responsibility and an opportunity to manage a marketing team. I am an energetic, industrious team-player, with excellent marketing skills, sound credit judgment, and a proven track record.

At your convenience, I would appreciate an opportunity to further discuss my capabilities and how best they can be utilized within your organization. In a few days I will call your secretary to set an appointment.

Sincerely,

Sample *Target Letter:*

Name
Title
Company
Address

Dear _____:

I am currently information systems manager for a year-long property reassessment project for the city of Stockton.

Because the project will be completed by the end of next month, I am seeking a new position in which my broad-based technical experience can be fully utilized. I have long been aware of your company's fine reputation and steady growth.

Recently, I read in Computer World of your aquisition of a large main-frame system, and plans to centralize your operation in a new data center in Merced. I believe that my special coordinating skills can be of value to you in the organization and management of such a large undertaking. I have been involved with several mainframe environments, and my familiarity with local networks can come in handy as you migrate from a local to a more central operation.

I will phone in a few days to arrange a meeting in which I can describe my background more fully and share with you some ideas I have for the rapid and efficient implementation of your project.

Sincerely,

Sample *Cover Letter to Search Firm:*

Name
Title
Company
Address

Dear _____:

If you are currently attempting to fill a responsible public relations or corporate communications position for one of your clients, you may find the enclosed resume of considerable interest.

At age 32, I am seeking immediate relocation and advancement, having attained nine years intensive and broad-based experience in key PR communications functions. An M.B.A. degree and more than five successful years with a major corporation in the media center of the nation are among my credentials.

While I prefer to relocate outside the New York metropolitan area, I am primarily seeking an opportunity for growth and advancement in my field: I will give full consideration to opportunities in internal or external communications functions and in consumer, service, or industrial sectors. My current salary, with bonus, is $55,000.

I look forward to discussing specific requirements of positions with your client organizations and will respond immediately to your call. Please feel free to call me at my office or my home.

Many thanks for your interest and consideration.

Sincerely,

Sample *Cover Letter to Search Firm:*

Name
Title
Company
Address

Dear _____:

Enclosed is a copy of my resume for your review.

I seek a position as a controller or vice president of finance with a small to medium-sized company.

My background includes fifteen years of financial experience, eleven of which have been in the retail industry and four in public accounting. I am 37 years old and have a B.S. degree in accounting from Brooklyn College.

Should you be recruiting for a financial executive in the $45,000–$50,000 salary range, please contact me. I would appreciate the opportunity of a personal interview to discuss my specific experience and abilities as they might fit your needs.

Sincerely yours,

Sample *Cover Letter to Search Firm:*

Name
Title
Company
Address

Dear _____:

In your search assignments, you may have a need for a professional sales/marketing executive with an outstanding record in both start-up and turnaround operations.

Having progressed up through the ranks from salesman to vice president marketing, my experience is with three companies of $100 million and up. Management responsibilities cover organizations of 10 to 250 people, with sales of $1.5 to $35 million.

Some of my accomplishments include:

- As part of a new management team at Burndy Corporation, brought a division from an $800,000 loss to a $1.5 million net profit in less than two years; during the 1974 recession, we increased corporate profits from five percent to seven percent net—in spite of a twenty-five percent industry-wide drop in electronic connector sales.
- Started a new division for Howell, Inc., establishing them among the top three companies in microfilm equipment and system sales; it is now their largest and most profitable product line.

The enclosed resume outlines my twenty-six-year growth record. I am currently seeking a position as v.p. marketing with an income of $60,000 to $70,00.

Cordially,

Strategies for the 90s

Out of Work and Other Unpleasantries
A Big Problem for the Nineties

If you are a good career planner, you should *never* be unemployed. Unemployment means you are unaware, a cardinal sin in career control. Never forget, the best way to get a job is to have one—one with significant accomplishments and personal references surrounding it.

Some folks, however, are nonetheless going to feel the corporate "boot" in the decade ahead. Corporate mergers, acquisitions, and job evolution will be happening with more frequency and at greater speed. So, if the "boot" hits your rear end, follow the job-search advice in this book, and you should substantially reduce your unemployment time.

If you are fired, the first situation you will face will be an emotional one: a sense of loss—of being homeless and unwanted. This is a time for family and friends to rally around you. You *must* immediately tell them what happened so you will receive the emotional support you need so desperately.

Next, make sure you have been properly treated by your former company. Adequate severance and continued benefits are a *must* if they don't want to see you in court. "Adequate" means *at least* one week of severance pay for every year of service—and that's if they are stingy. It will be two weeks for every year of service if their severance package is average. It will be three or more weeks for each year of service if they are generous. You decide, but those should be the ground rules.

Also, try to get your severance as "bridging-pay." This means that you stay on the payroll and receive your regular weekly, bi-monthly, or monthly paycheck for the period of the severance instead of a lump-sum payment. To the world, you are *still employed.* You will also have to negotiate a new title and responsibilities for the interim period. The title might be trouble-shooter in a certain area, or manager of a new research assignment. Whatever the title, try to negotiate for an office with a phone and secretarial help. Even though this scenario is a bit of a farce, believe us, it beats telling everyone you have been fired.

Of course, if you are not in a position to get a bridging-pay plan but are given a lump-sum severance instead, make sure you head for the unemployment office the next day. Don't be proud about this. You have earned it after all those years of paying into the fund! In most states, you will have a brief waiting-period after applying. A reminder: if you are receiving bridging-pay, you can't receive unemployment payments during that time, because you are still considered employed.

If you truly feel you have not been treated well, see a lawyer. But our advice is to use the lawyer *only* as a means of getting what's coming to you—a fair deal—if it wasn't offered upon termination. *Don't,* we repeat *don't,* go to court unless it is a very serious matter. Even then, we recommend that you get two or three legal opinions. Although you may hear about big settlements from sympathetic juries and judges, you have to understand the process and its cost to you, your family, and your career.

The court system is jammed and will continue to be through the next decade. In some cities, it takes three to five years to get into court. This means that your lawyer (and it had better be a contingency attorney, one who takes between thirty and fifty percent of any proceeds, rather than one who charges by the hour!) will probably want some up-front money sometime along the way to court. But the worst of it will be that you probably won't be working (or at least not on your career path) until the case is settled. That's because any company you approach will check with your former company, and you can bet your last buck that they will be told you are litigating.

So, since nobody wants a troublemaker, the upshot will be that you will be unemployed or underemployed for a very long time, hoping to win the litigation lottery. All the while, you will be having to feed a lawyer (who will *still* take a hefty amount of your winnings if you win). And even if you *do* prevail in court, think about the cost to you in terms of lost time on your intended career path!

No, better to put bitterness aside if the "boot" hits. If needed, let a lawyer bang the drums and rattle the swords for you with the company, but settle quickly and get on with your life and your *real* career.

Also, if job termination comes, and you have been in a senior position, ask for outplacement or career transition counseling. The company pays for it, and you will probably get an office from which to work, as well as secretarial services for letter writing and resume preparation. The counseling programs usually contain many of the same techniques and advice you will find in this book, but you will be personally coached by a trained career counselor who also knows the business world. You will get emotional support and a lot of good professional advice on how to conduct a job-search campaign. Such a program could significantly shorten your unemployment time and very well might help get you a raise (because you will be practiced and focused). So negotiate for this perk! If they don't give it to you in the initial severance package, go back in and ask for it later. Or, if need be, have your attorney negotiate it for you.

A tip: for heaven's sake, *don't*, we repeat *don't*, take the first job offered you, just because you and your family are frightened silly that you won't get another offer. If it is the right job, by all means go for it. But if it doesn't fit what you have decided is really what you want, WAIT! Better to take even a part-time job and wait for the *right* situation, than to be unfulfilled, less than fully productive, or even fail at something that is not really right.

And a little advance warning: you will have lots of ups and downs along the way. Just know they are coming, so that when they do you will recognize them for what they are—emotional blips. Some weeks you will receive all kinds of phone calls from your network—if you have organized it properly and maybe some mail from head-hunters and companies that want to see you. You will feel great! Then there will be those weeks when the phone doesn't ring even once, and the mail brings only bills and advertising flyers. You and your family will have that sinking feeling: "I'll never work again!" Of course then the process will reverse itself the next week. *Blips*—that's all they are, nothing else. Just know that they are part of the campaign, and don't do something drastic when the low blips happen, like taking the first job that comes along if it isn't the *right one*.

Another point. Don't say you were fired, are unemployed, or are out of work, even if it is the case. These statements indicate that you are a bad career planner. Couch your explanations by saying you had a difference in management style or personality conflicts with your boss and mutually decided to part company. Of course, decide what those differences or conflicts are—and rehearse how you describe them—before you talk to a head-hunter or a company executive. It's also a *must* to get agreement on these points with your former boss (or at least with the personnel department). Don't forget, the new company or head-hunter will probably phone for references.

One last thing. Don't bad-mouth your former employer or boss. That is always considered bad taste by any prospective employer, and it is bound to count against you.

In the coming decade:

"... **people should concentrate** on management skills: the ability to communicate effectively at all levels, both verbally and in written correspondence, and to be able to get those ideas or points across to whatever audience is being addressed. It is also important to develop a track record of creativity—demonstrated pro-active thinking—seeing a problem or opportunity and presenting an action plan to solve or take advantage of the situation."

• James J. Carter, Principal, Avery Crafts Associates Ltd.

CHAPTER SIX

SWEATY PALMS OR CUCUMBER COOL— IT'S INTERVIEW TIME!

Now it's the moment of truth. It's time to put it all together. It's SHOW TIME. So sell it!

A job interview is similar to a dance. Your partner is the interviewer, who will lead you through many steps—tough questions and issues with many hidden agendas. Unless you are knowledgeable about these steps, about how to follow the interviewer's lead as well as how to counter with a leading step yourself, you will get your feet (and tongue) all tangled up and probably fall down.

At the interview, you call upon everything you have done so far in the job-search process. You talk about your strengths, where you have worked, what you have accomplished, and what you want to do. You also *overlay* all of this information onto what you have discovered about the company in your research. Tell the interviewer what you can bring to the party, how you can

1. Help solve the organization's problems or resolve certain key issues.
2. Bring new ideas or change things in the company.
3. Reduce costs.
4. Increase sales and/or profits.

Overlaying is just like laying one piece of acetate over another on an overhead projector. One layer contains the company's problems and issues; the other contains what you can do about them.

This is a time to *sell,* not simply to be a "warm body" with sweaty palms and a dry mouth. Sell what you are and what you can do. And if you only remember one thing about interviewing, it should be a phrase similar to one said by President Kennedy: "Talk not about what the company can do for you; talk about what you can do for the company." That will get you the job.

There is a simple formula we suggest you keep in mind during your interviews. It will keep you on track and doing all the right things:

$$Q = A + P \text{ (Questions} = \text{Answer} + \text{Probe)}$$

In other words, when you are asked a question, answer it and then probe—ask why the interviewer asked the question; explore all sides of the question as to the company's needs, problems, and plans. This is what will make you look good in an interview!

What Are They Really Looking For in an Interview?

Basically, interviewers are trying to find out (1) if you can do the job, (2) if you match the company's image, (3) if you will fit in the department, and (4) if the salary amount is right for you.

To gather this information, they ask all kinds of questions, each with an eye to both your personal and accomplishment profiles. The personal profile encompasses your confidence, energy, enthusiasm, poise, reliability, dedication, creativity, aggressiveness, and skills in communication and analysis. The accomplishment profile includes the ideas, procedures, and systems you have developed; your problem-solving and organizational skills; the money and time you have saved (efficiency), and the profits you have earned.

A candidate "must first be *absolutely* presentable: shined shoes, no wrinkled shirt or blouse. Their first impact must be

exceptional, even if the H.R. person or hiring manager is not 100 percent presentable. Everybody wants a person who is a cut above. The candidate should also be very inquisitive and ask a lot of questions about the company—its values, culture, goals, etc. Taking notes is a plus in my book. Also, *never* bad-mouth previous bosses or employers."

> • Vera Blanchet, Vice President/Human Resources, Corporate Headquarters, California Federal Savings & Loan Association

---

I Am Always a Bundle of Nerves in Interviews. How Can I Get Over This?

You can overcome your nervousness by concentrating on the self-confidence you have developed from having done your homework and therefore knowing you are prepared. You have researched the company; you know yourself (your skills and accomplishments), and you have thought through your answers to most of the questions that will be asked. Many of these questions can be found at the end of this chapter.

You are also on time for the interview (not late, having researched how to get there and how long the trip takes), and you know that you are dressed appropriately.

You have brought a list of questions you want to ask, and you know what salary and benefits you want, as well as how to negotiate for them.

Now then, take three deep breaths, and go in there to knock 'em dead.

How Will I Know What Kind of Interview They Are Planning for Me?

You probably won't, so be *ready* for any one of several types.

Screening interview: the initial step, sometimes on the phone, sometimes a first meeting with the human resources department. Its purpose is nearly always to determine your basic qualifications for a particular job, as well as your salary needs. Your goal is to get past this, to the. . .

Selection interview: the second step, sometimes with another human resources person, sometimes with the potential boss, sometimes with a member of the boss's staff. These interviews can include very pointed questions about your experience and accomplishments, to find out if you fit pre-determined skill qualifications, or they can be a series of general, indirect questions to see if you fit in with a department's culture. But watch out, because in the selection interview, you may meet the dragon—the . . .

Stress interview: a generally unpleasant experience (from your viewpoint), designed to see how you react under pressure to very specific, pointed, rapid-fire questions. There's not much you can do in one of these interviews except answer the questions as best you can—the interviewer usually doesn't let you ask many questions. However, if you have done your homework, you should be able to survive in reasonably good shape, unless pressure is not your "thing" in which case, tell them so!

What interview style works best for a candidate?

"**Eclectic.** Interviewers are as different as snowflakes. Applicants should adjust their style to the interviewer's mood or personality. If, for example, the interviewer is reserved, the candidate should put on a conservative demeanor. I like to cover the basics like why they are here, what they want to do, what education and experience they bring to us, and what their expectations are as employees. If the applicant tells me most of this in the course of conversation, they get points. If I have to probe too much to get answers to these basic questions, I may get the impression that either what I want is too simple or the applicant is too simple."

• Doug Cooper, Vice President/Personnel,
Valero Energy Corporation

"Conversational. An interview is an exchange of information, not an interrogation."
 • John Regan, Corporate Employment Programs Manager, Digital Equipment Corporation

"Define your own style and stick to it, but modify it toward a middle range. Above all, be enthusiastic, ask questions, and be clear about what you have done and what you can do."
 • Peggy Foster, Human Resources Consultant

How Do I Start Off? Do I Let the Interviewer Lead the Conversation?

Generally, you will start with some small talk about the weather, the traffic, a sports or TV event, or else the interviewer will lead with one of these topics. Of course, there is always the chance that you will meet a genuine introvert who is more nervous than you could ever be. So always have something in mind to open with, just in case.

Next, you will get down to business with a question from the interviewer such as, "Tell me about yourself." (About eighty percent of all interviews start with this one, so have a good response!) This is not a good time to attempt humor: "Well, I was born at a very early age . . ." or to be lengthy with your whole life story—how many interviewers have mentally slept through this stuff! Instead, have an overview statement memorized, describing your career path and job interests. It is a good idea to hand your resume to the interviewer at this point, since it will spark further questions about you. From here, you will talk about your skills, experience, and accomplishments.

The next phase should consist of you leading the conversation with questions about the company and its goals and environment, as well as the job and its responsibilities and objectives. You will also want to find out about authority, span of control, budgets, and the former incumbent in the job—what happened to the person, did he or she succeed, and why or why not.

Lastly, you will have a give-and-take about how your skills and
accomplishments overlay the job's requirements and the company's
needs. You will also want to get a sense from the interviewer about
whether there *is* a match. If there is, another interview should be
offered (or you should ask for it) and/or an offer should be made.

So the interview process is really a two-way street, with the conversation changing as the various phases progress.

Some Interviewers Are Pretty Clever with Their Hidden Agenda Questions. How Do I Know When I Am Being Set Up?

Be aware. Keep your antennae up and keep sniffing the air. Interviewing is a lot like playing a card game such as poker or bridge. In a
card game, you must always stay aware of what cards have been
played. In interviewing, you must always remember what questions
have been asked and always try to link them (a process similar to
threading to find your strengths, etc.).

A classic example of an aware interviewee who linked questions
was a client of ours who phoned after an interview to tell us how
proud he was of himself for finding a very important hidden agenda.
The interviewer was the vice president of manufacturing for a company with several plants outside the United States, and he was looking for a plant manager for their facility in a Middle East country. The
v.p. began by asking our friend if he liked the natives of that country.
Our friend said he had no problems with these people but asked,
"Why the question?" No reply. Several minutes passed with other
questions, and then the v.p. asked, "How many people have you
hired, and how many have you fired?" Our friend responded with
the number and asked if there was to be a reorganization at the plant.
No reply—question avoided. Several more minutes passed then:
"Are you a drinker?" Our friend responded by saying he enjoyed
spirits occasionally, but in moderation. "Why do you ask?" Again, no
answer. Next: "Can you work alone, with little support from the
home office?"

By now, our friend had grown suspicious and had begun to link
some questions together. More minutes passed, and finally the v.p.

"I can assure you that, as a lifelong underachiever, I pose no threat to your employees."

asked, "Have you ever gone through bankruptcy?" An illegal question, but more importantly, it completed the puzzle. By then, our friend had come up with a pretty clear picture of the v.p.'s hidden agenda, which, incidentally, later proved to be completely accurate.

Evidently, the former Middle East plant manager had been out there all alone, received little or no support from this v.p., and had developed a drinking problem. His excessive drinking led to financial problems that eventually resulted in bankruptcy. Had our friend not linked questions by staying aware, he might have taken the job and suffered the same fate as his predecessor.

Moral: stay aware and *probe*. Don't be bashful. If a question seems odd or ambiguous, simply ask why it was asked. Or, "What do you mean?" or "How does that question relate to this job?" Pursue this tactic, and you will spot where the aces are hidden!

How Much Detail Should I Give about My Background?

As much as the interviewer wants to hear. Again, stay alert and take your cue from the questions being asked. Begin answering each question with the essential facts. If the interviewer wants more detail, he or she will ask for it. But *don't overtalk;* don't get into all the nitty-gritty before you know that is what is wanted.

Also, as you answer questions and give detail about your accomplishments, *overlay* these accomplishments onto the job you are seeking. For instance, if you are interviewing for a job selling computers and you have been doing that for another company, you might describe the sales strategy you used to sell a particular account, mentioning that you could use the same strategy to gain access to certain other accounts for the new company. Tell them how you would do it, why you would do it, and what the results could be. But be concise and offer only as much detail as seems needed.

Or, if you work in the operations department of a utility and you are interviewing with another utility, describe how you solved a particularly troublesome problem, saving "x" number of manhours and thus "x" number of dollars. The utility with which you are interviewing may have similar problems, and you can solve them, right? Tell them how, why, and what the results might be.

In short, keep it short, unless you are asked to do otherwise. Be forceful, confident, and direct. If you have researched the company thoroughly, you have probably identified some of their problems; these are their hot buttons and exactly the ones you want to push.

An advertiser may be able to sell "the sizzle, not the steak," but you have to sell both. The "sizzle" is the interviewer's perception of you as a person: your body language, your personality, your energy level. The "steak" is the substance of your accomplishments, your skills and experience. Nobody wants to hire just a "warm body." Get in there and tell them who you are and what you can do for them!

How can any candidate maximize his or her chances of being hired?

- *Appropriate* networking.
- Good *listening* skills and appropriate responses.

• Good attitude: not too cocky nor too quiet.
     • Beverly Fuentes, Vice President/Staffing and
      Employment, Bank of America

"**Have an accurate** and current resume.
Be punctual.
Dress appropriately for the position.
Be familiar with the company and its product.
Be direct with all answers.
Don't use slang; use proper and grammatically correct
English.
Ask questions.
Don't prolong the interview unnecessarily."
    • Joe Wegener, Vice President/Personnel,
     A.P.I. Alarm Systems

What Do I Do When that Awful, Awkward "Silent Moment" Comes, and Nobody Knows What To Say?

This awkward moment *can* happen, particularly with inexperienced interviewers. The best remedy is for you to speak up and ask one of the questions that you brought in with you. That will get the conversation going again, and you will learn a little more about the company.

Incidentally, sometimes you can use the silent pause to your advantage. Let's say you have been trying to obtain more information about a particular issue or subject but, for some reason, the interviewer has simply not been responding. Ask another pointed question about the subject, then keep quiet. There will be an awkward, silent pause, and the interviewer may try to "un-awkward" the moment by talking more about the subject, maybe even giving you the details you need. Sometimes silence *can* be golden, but you have to know how to use it.

If I Ask Too Many Questions, Won't They Think I Am Prying into the Company's Business?

Absolutely not! And if they do, you had better wonder about what they are hiding and why. You have every right to ask all the questions you wish. After all, it's your *career* that we are talking about here, one of the most important aspects of your life! You certainly don't want to make a mistake and take a job before you know as much about it as is reasonably possible.

Actually, interviewers usually respect the candidate who asks a lot of questions. It shows intelligence, curiosity, and concern and demonstrates that you took the time to prepare for the interview by doing research and compiling a list of questions.

Your questions should be probing, however, not simply idle chatter. They should all start with one of these words: why, how, who, what, where, or when. "Why is the company building its new plant here?" or "What were the company's net earnings on sales last year?"

Yes, probe away. Ask and ye shall find (and maybe get the job!).

What Kinds of Questions Should I Ask in an Interview?

As we have said, your questions should be probing. They should be designed to help you evaluate the company, to see that it matches *your* needs. Remember the "happy sheet" exercise in the chapter on self-assessment? Now is the time you find out if the top four elements in each of the three categories exist in the company. If they *do*, you will be a happy and productive employee.

So ask about each of the twelve "happy sheet" elements you have chosen. Also ask the following:

1. What are the responsibilities and budget accountabilities of the position?
2. How will I be evaluated, and in what time frames? What performance standards will be used?
3. What is the history of the position? How has it been managed previously, and what happened to the previous incumbent?

4. How well is the position defined? Can its scope of authority and responsibility be expanded or changed?
5. Does the job entail profit-and-loss responsibility?
6. What mission statement has been agreed upon for the department and company, and are they likely to change?
7. Where can I go from here in the company, presuming I exceed the job's accountabilities and the company's expectations?
8. With whom would I be working? Who would be my supervisor, and what is his or her background? Who would my peers be, and whom would I supervise? What is the department's atmosphere or environment like?
9. What are the company's sales and growth rate? Who are the company's competitors and customers (if you have been unable to find this information through your research)?
10. When will a decision be made about this position?
11. What is the next step in the decision-making process?

Don't be afraid to ask these questions, as well as any questions regarding your "happy sheet" or anything else. The interviewer will respect your initiative and concern.

Is There A Way I Can Quickly Grab the Advantage at the Start of an Interview?

Sure! Begin the business part of the conversation with *your* questions first. For instance, when you sense there has been enough small talk after meeting the interviewer, you can say something like, "Before we get started, may I ask one or two questions of you?" That way, you will quickly gain the advantage by taking the initiative.

Do First Impressions Count for Much in Interviews?

You bet they do! The chemistry between you and the interviewer is usually established during the first few moments. If it's good chemistry, there is a strong chance you will be viewed as a good candidate for the job. If the chemistry is bad, chances are the interviewer will feel uncomfortable and may try to cut short the interview.

So, you will want to be aware of several factors that create good first impressions:

1. A neat appearance.
2. A firm handshake—no limp fish, but no vice grips either.
3. Good eye contact. Make sure you look the interviewer in the eye frequently, but don't stare.
4. Proper body language. Sit up straight, express a positive attitude, and don't use excessive hand gestures.
5. Listen. Above all, listen to the interviewer's questions, and answer them crisply and to the point. Don't ramble.

"Competitive pressures are forcing companies to be more thorough in the selection process. Organizations worldwide cannot afford 'mis-hires.' Research that Smart & Associates has conducted indicates that the estimated cost of mis-hiring a person is two to four times the person's annual compensation. The result: much more in-depth interviews and reference checks. The job-seeker must prepare for in-depth interviews and assume that only a very honest approach to interviewing will suffice, since very thorough reference-checking will be performed."
• Dr. Brad Smart, President, Smart & Associates, Inc.

Should I Always Dress Up for an Interview?

Not necessarily. You should, however, dress appropriately. If you are seeking an office job, from company president to secretary or clerk, it is a good idea for men to wear a suit or sports jacket and a tie, and for women to wear a suit or dress (not a cocktail dress!). If you do technical or production work, you may wear whatever is appropriate to your business.

Whatever you do, don't wear loud colors or lots of jewelry (men or women). Also, avoid the heavy use of perfume or cologne. In most cases, it is best to play it on the conservative side.

Unlawful Questions—What Are They?

Unlawful questions differ slightly from state to state and from the federal to the state level, but most attorneys and experts in the field prescribe to guidelines set up by the state of New York. These questions are usually asked in a pre-employment interview or on a pre-employment application. Although it is complicated and difficult to prove, many questions (or the answers provided) can be used for discriminatory purposes. And that is, needless to say, highly illegal. Here is a list of subjects and questions that are considered unlawful to ask, either on a pre-employment application or during a pre-employment interview.

1. Race or color: any question.
2. Religion or creed: any question.
3. National origin: any question involving nationality of parents or spouse or involving your native language.
4. Marital status: any questions, including how you wish to be addressed (Mr., Mrs., Miss, or Ms.), name or other information about your spouse, or the ages of your children, if any.
5. Birth control: any question, including capacity to reproduce or advocacy of birth control or family planning.
6. Age or birthdate: how old you are, or what your birthdate is. Also any reference to birth certificate, baptismal record, etc.
7. Disability: whether you have a disability, or whether you have ever been treated "for the following diseases."
8. Arrest record: whether you have ever been arrested. It is lawful to be asked if you have ever been convicted of a crime.
9. Birthplace: any questions, including questions about the birthplace of your parents, spouse, or other close relative.
10. Photograph: none may be required.
11. Citizenship: only a question as to whether you are a U.S. citizen may be asked. If you are not, you may be legally asked if you intend to become one, and if you have a legal right to remain in the United States.

12. Language: any questions as to your native language, or about
    how you learned to read, write, or speak a foreign language.
13. Relatives: names, addresses, ages or other information about
    relatives, spouse, or children *not* employed by the company.
14. Organizations: any requirement to list clubs, societies, or
    lodges to which you belong.

These questions are considered unlawful *only* in *pre-employment* interviews and applications. After hiring, you can be asked several of
these questions, as the information may be needed for insurance,
health benefits, pension plans, and other job-related reasons.

How Should I React to an Unlawful Question?

Your first reaction should be to realize that the interviewer does not
know the law—and the discrimination laws are *not* new! So that tells
you something about the person's awareness and perhaps that of the
company as well.

In responding to an unlawful question, it is probably best not to
call the person on it in a threatening way. That may only blow the job
opportunity by angering or embarrassing the interviewer. Instead,
you may want to joke about it with something like, "Do I look like
I've been arrested?" or "Do I look like I'm not an American?" If your
answer can't hurt you, you may choose, depending on the situation,
to answer the question, unlawful or not. You may then want to say
something like, "Didn't I read that that's a no-no in an interview?"
Make your remarks as off-handed as possible. The interviewer will
get the point—that you know the law.

Is There Any Legal Recourse if I Am Asked an Unlawful Question and, as a Result, Feel That I Have Been Discriminated Against?

Yes, there is. But be careful, it *could* cost you a lot of money if discrimination is not proven.

If you feel you have been discriminated against because of an illegal question asked in a pre-employment interview, you should file a charge within the allowed filing time with your state agency handling these issues. These agencies have differing names from state to state. The filing requirements and remedies taken by various state agencies differ, so it is best to check with your state agency.

You should also file a charge concurrently with the Federal Equal Employment Opportunity Commission (EEOC) within 180 days of the occurrence. You do not need a lawyer to file with either the state agency or the EEOC.

If the EEOC does *not* find reasonable cause for your claim, you will be so advised and informed of your right to sue independently. You can then see an attorney if you wish. If the EEOC *does* find reasonable cause for your claim, it will try for an agreement with the company as to remedy. If an agreement is not reached, the EEOC may file suit, or it may issue you a right-to-sue letter. You have ninety days to file your own suit after you receive this letter.

If you cannot afford an attorney, all you need do is file your right-to-sue letter in federal court within ninety days of receipt and apply for an appointment of counsel.

If you have your own attorney, and if you win the case, part of the settlement will cover your attorney's fees. But if you lose—and here is where it gets sticky—you may have to pay the defendant's attorney's fees! So, be absolutely certain that the unlawful question was asked of you for the purpose of *discrimination* before committing to litigation.

When a Company Calls One of My References, What Will They Ask?

First of all, remember not to offer references until they are asked for, not before. If and when the company checks out your references, they will probably ask any or all of the following questions.

1. How long did you work for or with the candidate?
2. What was the quality of his or her work?

"Do you have any references, Miss Baxter, who *aren't* deceased?"

3. What responsibilities did he or she have?
4. What were some of his or her accomplishments?
5. How well does he or she get along with people?
6. Was he or she punctual?
7. How much supervision did he or she require?
8. Is there anything that might disqualify him or her for the prospective job?

9. Why did he or she leave your company?
10. Is there anyone else who could speak about him or her?

The last question is, of course, a way to reach people whom you have not prompted or preconditioned. Interviewers know that you are not going to give them a reference who will give you a "bad rap." This tactic is their way around that problem.

But Since I Am New to the Job Scene (a Recent High-School or College Grad, or a Woman Entering or Re-Entering the Job Market After Raising a Family), I Won't Have Much To Say about Accomplishments or Responsibilities, Will I?

Oh, yes you will! From school, you will have your grades and your extra-curricular activities (such as sports, the band, or clubs) to talk about, highlighting your leadership roles and accomplishments. You don't need to have been the star jock of the school either. Maybe you were simply treasurer or cashier for the school play, but you accounted for every dime! Or perhaps you were membership chairman for the book club and increased its members by "x" percent, or you were travel manager for the school band and solved several sticky situations. These accomplishments all demonstrated your skills, and you can overlay these skills onto a company's problems or issues.

If you are a mom entering or re-entering the work force, you have a lot to talk about! You have been quite an operations manager of the home: budgeteer, dietician, travel manager, amateur psychologist, etc, etc. Think back about some of the thorny problems you have solved successfully. Think about them, and discuss them with your family; make a list and analyze each accomplishment in terms of the skill or talent necessary to achieve the desired results.

What Are Some of the Reasons I Would Be Rejected for a Job?

There are, of course, many. Some reasons might stem from the fact that you interviewed poorly; some might be related to other issues. Here is a check list. Look it over and make sure *you* are not the cause of your rejection.

YOUR FAULT:
Poor appearance.
Unrealistic demands about the job or salary.
Too little knowledge about the company.
Talking too much or too little in the interview.
Being overly clever or coy, or using tasteless humor.
Being too modest.
Not following up after the interview.
Your references didn't check out.
NOT YOUR FAULT (You can't do much about these.):
An insider is chosen.
A better candidate shows up.
The position isn't or hasn't been approved by higher authority.
A freeze on hiring.
A merger or takeover threat.
You didn't meet the decision-maker.
Enough money wasn't allocated in the budget.

Can I Fib Just a Little in Talking about My Accomplishments, as Well as My Salary?

Better not. It is too easy to check on whatever you say, and then you will be eliminated from any consideration for the job. Tell it like it is, even with salary, if you must! They may ask for a W-2 form from your current or former employer. If you lied, you are in the soup, right? Be honest. It is always the best policy, and it lets you sleep at night as well.

What Should I Take to an Interview?

1. A pad of paper and a pen or pencil. Yes, it is okay to take notes; the interviewer will, and you should too.
2. Information about the company you are interviewing, taken from your research.
3. At least three copies of your resume. You never know who will want one.
4. The phone number of the interviewer in case you are delayed on the way.

5. Your list of references.
6. Your list of questions about the job and company.

Will I Ever Be Interviewed on the Phone? If So, How Should I Handle It?

Yes, you may be interviewed on the phone, usually in one of the following three scenarios.

1. You may be networking on the phone and find yourself in an interview either because (1) the person with whom you are talking wants to be sure of you and your qualifications before referring you to a friend or (2) the person has a job that fits your objective.
2. A company may call you as a result of a resume you mailed.
3. You may have set up an initial screening interview by phone, or a personnel agency may have set one up for you.

When a phone interview happens, you *must* do four things to make it successful.

1. Get the listener's attention by briefly describing your career background (what you have been doing and where). If you have initiated the call, you might add, "Have I caught you at a good time?" (*Never* say "a bad time.") If it is not a good time, ask when would be a good time to talk.
2. Gain the listener's interest by describing your accomplishments.
3. Create a desire to know more about you by saying that you are looking for a new opportunity, have done some research, and have found the person's company to be interesting.
4. Make the person take action by asking if your skills and accomplishments are what that company is looking for.

Telephone interviews are not easy, since you can't see the other person's reactions, but they can get you an in-person interview if you handle them properly.

On the Phone, I Get Lots of "Put-Off" Responses. How Can I Turn These into Interviews?

The most common "put-off" responses are the following:

"Send me your resume." If you get this response, say you will be glad to send a resume, but in order to know if your qualifications fit their needs, you would like to know what skills and experience they are looking for in the position. That should get the person talking and may get you in for an in-person chat.

"I'm too busy to talk." Reply by asking what the best time would be for you to phone again, perhaps early morning or late afternoon? Or suggest that since you are going to be in that part of town tomorrow, why not come by to see the person then—what is his or her quietest time? That may get you in the door.

"You should see the personnel department." Respond by asking who in personnel you should see; then ask if there is a particular position open. This will at least tie down whether there *is* an opportunity. It will also give you an introduction to personnel and may get you in to see the person with whom you are talking.

"We only promote from within." Your answer should indicate that you realize this is their policy, and it is one reason why you are interested in the company. You are also bright and talented. When they do hire from the outside, what skills and experience do they look for? You now have a chance to overlay your skills onto the company's needs and to call the person's bluff. Plus if you sell yourself well enough, you may get an interview.

"We're not hiring now." Ask what they look for when they *do* hire; then overlay your experience onto those qualities. Also ask about problems or situations they are facing. Perhaps you have researched a few. They may end up hiring now after all.

After an Interview, Should I Follow Up with the Company or Wait To Hear from Them?

The early bird gets the worm. Be assertive (not aggressive) and *always* send a thank-you or follow-up letter within twenty-four hours of an interview to each person that interviewed you. First of all, that is simply the gracious thing to do. Secondly, it gives you a chance to do a little more selling.

The letter should always include your appreciation of the person's time and courtesy, a summary of the discussion (job duties, environment, reporting relationships, etc.), a reference to the overlay you established as to your skills and the company's problems, and your enthusiasm for the challenge you perceive in the job.

This letter is also a chance to voice any of those issues that ran through your mind after the interview was over and left you with that nagging "Oh my God, I forgot to mention . . ." feeling.

How Often Should I Follow Up on a Job Prospect After Interviewing?

You should certainly follow up as often as they suggest—or as often as you feel is right. But don't follow up too frequently, as that might put you in a position of looking too anxious. Trust your intuition on this one.

Interview or interview requests should be followed up:

"**Weekly for a known opening.** Thirty days for a general inquiry with no response. Always follow up after an interview with an expression of interest and any follow-up questions."
   • Thomas J. Haines, Corporate Director, Human Resources, Fairchild Industries, Inc

---

"**weekly.** After four follow-ups, one could assume that an interview is not likely. After the interview, write a thank-you letter. I have never known an interviewer who was not impressed with this gesture. Call within three days after the thank-you before the interviewer forgets about being impressed."
   • Doug Cooper, Vice President/Personnel, Valero Energy Corporation

How Frequently Should a Candidate Follow Up
After an Interview?

"**As a rule of thumb,** once after a first interview. Beyond that, pressing just becomes counterproductive.

As to the decision, it partially depends on how the interview(s) ended. A good recruiter will give a general time frame for response and a follow up would be appropriate when that has lapsed. (Naturally, an acknowledgement or thank you after the interview(s) is always appropriate.) A lengthy period between interview(s) and response is normally not a good sign. After one or two attempts at follow up, I would leave the ball in the company's court and move on to the next option."
• Olon P. Zager, Director of Human Resources, Gucci

"**Ask when** the decision will be made. Call again to indicate interest and/or if you have another offer and must make a choice."
• John L. Hanson, Vice President/Human Resources, Parker Hannifin Corporation

If I Have Had Another Job Offer, Should I Mention It during My Follow-Up Call?

You can certainly mention it, but *no* details. Never reveal other company names or people you are dealing with. You never know who knows whom or what can happen if those folks talk. Keep it all confidential.

If I Am Turned Down for a Job I Really Want, Should I Just Forget It and Move On to Other Opportunities?

Absolutely not! If an interviewer (or several of them) *erroneously* conclude that you are not the right person for the job, there are ways to salvage the situation. Of course, realistically, no one is right for *every* position, but if you have done your homework (your research and preparation for the interview), you probably should be right for the job. So your rejection indicates that a glitch has occurred somewhere in the interview process. Chances are, either the interviewer felt that you could not do the job or that your personality would not fit the department. So, whether by phone, by mail, or in person

1. Thank the interviewer for his or her time. Then ask, for purposes of your continued job search, why you were not chosen? Listen carefully, take notes and *don't interrupt or argue.* After you have learned why, tell the interviewer that you certainly can understand his or her position but that "interview nerves" got in the way. Ask if you may meet with him or her once again. Say that this time, when you are not so nervous, you are sure you will be able to show that you have the skills for the job. Ask when would be a good time for another interview, and make sure you end with this question. With this enthusiastic approach, you are likely to be given another chance. If you succeed . . .

2. Go back over your research material about the company, and do your overlays. Re-read the annual report and make sure you know about their facilities, their sales and earnings, products, and competitors, as well as what the president and/or chairman's report(s) said, etc.

3. Rehearse your practice questions and answers with a family member or friend You already know some of these from the first rounds. You might even consider renting a TV camera and playback unit in order to check out your performance.

4. Get back in there with enthusiasm, thank the person for this second chance, and give the performance of your life.

5. Even if all else has failed, end with a statement that you would like to prove your worthiness on the job. Will he or she please give you the opportunity?

We have seen this technique work time after time. It is hard to say no to this kind of persistence.

What Questions Can I Expect at an Interview?

It would be impossible to cover all of the possibilities, but we are going to list many of them here, with hints as to how you might answer them. These are not word-for-word answers you should memorize. That won't work—you will never remember our answers in the fast-paced give-and-take of an actual interview. One suggestion is to use our hints about an answer to create *your own* personal answer, and then practice, practice, practice. Again, use a family member or friend to help you conduct a practice session. So, here are some sample questions. Some questions we just list in order to get you thinking; for most of them we also provide comments and possible responses.

"Tell me about yourself." This is probably, far and away, the most common interview starter. Give the interviewer a copy of your resume and say, "As you can see from my resume, I've worked for (so and so) company(s) and I've been involved in (so and so) functions. What would you like me to talk about first?" This question will cause the interviewer to pick a company or function for you to talk about. Remember the equation "Q = A + P?" Answer the question and then probe—ask the interviewer about the company's current problems or issues, and then overlay your past experience and skills onto those problems or issues. Try to focus on what *you* can do for the employer.

"Are you a competitive person?" It is best to indicate that you are a team player, but you *do* compete against yourself.

"You've changed jobs frequently. Why?" Talk about better opportunity and more money. Focus on more challenge in each job.

"Give me examples of your creativity, as well as your analytical, administrative, and leadership skills." Be prepared with two or three examples of each, probably from your resume accomplishments.

"How do you motivate people?" You find their "hot buttons" and press them.

"What kinds of people attract you, and what kinds of people annoy you?" Positive, bright, creative people attract you. Negative, unmotivated, poorly-groomed people annoy you.

"Why are you leaving your present company?" You are seeking more challenge for your skills.

"Have you ever been fired?" This one is tricky, and they can check on it, so don't lie! If the answer is yes, you might want to couch it in terms such as the following: "My boss and I had different styles

and personalities—we were like oil and water. The parting was inevitable." Whatever you do, *Don't* bad-mouth the boss or the company!

"Have you ever considered self-employment?" Better say you prefer the give-and-take—"Interface" is sometimes used—of a larger organization.

"How would you describe your ideal boss?" Tell it like it is.

"Do you prefer working with others or independently?" Unless your objective is clearly one or the other, better pick a middle-of-the-road position here.

"How do you spend your free time?" Talk about personal growth issues, such as sports and physical fitness, school, reading, as well as family and friends.

"What are your travel and/or relocation limitations?" Be prepared to tell them like it is—no sense getting into a problem later.

"How should people criticize you, and how do you criticize others?" You like positive, constructive criticism, and you give the same. The first part of this question may be an attempt to discover your weaknesses. Don't fall for it!

"Could you have done more in your last job?" Of course you could. Admit it, and give a couple of "in retrospect" examples.

"How could you have improved your career progress?" Think this one out carefully; don't be caught flat-footed.

"When did you last experience anger on the job and why?" Indicate that your anger was in response to someone's negativity, tardiness, or lack of commitment, etc.

"How do you organize projects?" Again, think this out before you are faced with it.

"What have you done lately that you considered a little crazy?" Don't go overboard here; be conservative.

"How many hours per week do you think someone should spend on the job?" Be very careful here. If you say "as many as necessary," you may be asked to put in fifty, sixty, or even seventy "necessary" hours per week. It might be better to say between forty and fifty hours per week. More than that means the job needs reevaluation and perhaps more people to do it.

"What do you know about the company?" Be prepared with some

information about such things as products, size, sales, profit, reputation, image, goals, problems, management talent, management style, people, skills, history, and philosophy. Don't say you don't know much; state that you would like to know more.

"Why do you want to work for us?" Mention a company project you would like to be part of or a company problem you think you can help solve. Describe some contribution you think you can make to specific company goals.

"What can you do for us that someone else can't?" Relate past success in solving previous employer problems that may be similar to those of the prospective employer.

"What do you find most attractive about our job opening?" Mention the challenge of the assignment and the opportunity to achieve results.

"Why should we hire you?" Cite a need you can fill. Refer to your relevant skills.

"What do you look for in a job?" Include opportunities to use your specific abilities and to increase and develop your skills.

"Please give me your definition of a _____(the position for which you are being interviewed)." Think this out carefully.

"How long would it take you to make a meaningful contribution to our firm?" Don't undersell or oversell yourself. If you can convert immediate task responsibility into meaningful contributions, do so. You might say, for example, "It may take some months before I can . . . but . . ."

"You may be overqualified or too experienced for the position we have to offer." Possible answers include: "A strong company needs a strong person." "Experienced executives are at a premium today." "A growing, energetic company is rarely unable to use the talents of its employees." Emphasize interest in long-term association. Say that the employer will get a faster return on investment because you have more experience than required.

"What is your philosophy of management?" If you have never thought about this, it is high time you did.

"What is your management style?" Refer to your abilities to set goals, to chart objectives, and to draw up and implement action plans.

Mention as well that you encourage participative management by getting input from your staff.

"As a manager, what did you look for when you hired people?" Refer to skills, initiative, adaptability.

"As a manager, did you ever fire anyone? If so, what were the reasons, and how did you handle it?" You tried to be as helpful as possible.

"What do you see as a manager's or executive's most difficult task?" A good answer might be: "Getting things planned and done through the efforts of others."

"What important trends do you see in our industry?" If you are a novice in the industry, don't fake it.

"What are the 'frontier' issues of your profession?" Be direct. Don't get up on a soapbox.

"Describe what you feel to be an ideal working environment." Study your answers in self-assessment chapter.

"How would you evaluate the firm you are currently working for?" Be balanced. State both negatives and positives.

"Have you helped increase sales? Profits? How?"

"Have you helped reduce costs? How?"

"How much money did you ever account for?"

"How many people did you supervise on your last job?"

"In your current or last position, what features did you like most? Least?"

"What are your five most significant accomplishments in your current or last position? In your career so far?" Memorize these.

"Have you thought of leaving your present position before? If yes, what do you think held you back?"

"Would you describe a few situations in which your work was criticized?" Demonstrate how you turn criticism into an opportunity to learn and improve.

"Can you work under pressure?" This may be a hidden-agenda question. Probe.

"How have you changed the nature of your job?"

"Do you prefer staff or line work? Why?"

"In your present position, what problems have you identified that had previously been overlooked?"

"What salary do you expect if we can offer this position to you?" Be careful. The market value of the job may be the key answer. For example: "My understanding is that a job like the one you are describing may be in the range of $_____."

"What kind of salary are you worth?" You'd better be worth at least what the job pays. Research!

"Any objections to psychological tests?" There is no use debating this. If you are willing to take the tests, why put up a red flag about your reservations?

"What other types of jobs and companies are you considering?" Be careful here.

"How would you describe your own personality?" Be balanced, but essentially focus on the positive.

"Are you a leader?" Give examples. Point out that most positions require both the ability to lead (take initiative, set a model) and to follow (respond to needs and directives).

"What are your goals?" Avoid statements such as "I would like the job you advertised." Instead, give long-range goals. Relate your answer to the employer rather than giving a self-serving reply: "In a firm such as yours, I would like to be . . ." not "I am so capable, I should be . . ."

"What are your strong points?" Present at least three. Relate them to the interviewing company and job opening.

"What are your weak points?" Don't say you don't have any. Turn a negative into a positive answer. For example, "I am sometimes impatient and do the work myself when we are late."

"Would you object to working for a woman?" Answer "No."

"What position do you expect to have in five years?" Respond in terms of objectives (responsibilities, accomplishments) rather than job titles. For example: "A job in which I can . . ."

"What are you doing, or what have you done, to reach those objectives?" Give yourself credit.

"How would you describe the essence of success?" Talk about success as being able to know when a new direction is needed, and having the initiative and courage to take it.

How Can I Critique My Interview Performance?

Easy! After each job interview, use the following questions to evaluate how well you performed. Build up your *self*-observation skills by responding to these questions after each interview.

1. Do you feel good about how it went?
2. What did you do or say that particularly pleased you?
3. What did you do or say that you think needs improvement?
4. Did you listen, without interrupting, to what the company or boss needed?
5. What questions were asked that you think you need more practice in answering?
6. Did you articulate your relevant talents, skills, and experience?
7. Did you create an opportunity to communicate your accomplishments?
8. Did you, by words and manner, create a positive picture?
9. Did you stick to relevant issues without rambling?
10. Was your voice firm and strong?
11. What phase of the interview was easiest for you?
12. What phase of the interview was hardest for you?
13. Were you at ease?
14. Is the job described one you would be interested in securing?
15. Did you leave with an atmosphere of mutual respect and regard?
16. Did the interviewer like you? How do you know?
17. Is there a plan for you to come back?
18. What follow-up steps would be appropriate?

Which interview styles work best for candidates?

"**Inquisitive and aggressive.** I like to let the candidate know about the company and the job. I expect them to ask questions. I then want them to tell me how their background is comparable to what I need. I don't expect them to have to pull information from

me. I want to feel they are comfortable and familiar, but not
cocky."

> • Vera Blanchet, Vice President/Human Resources,
> California Federal Savings & Loan Association

Strategies for the 90s

Women in Business

"In the United States, forty-five percent of our company's total
work force is women, and twenty-three percent of our
management positions are held by women. . . . I don't think it is
enough."

> • R. Gordon McGovern, Chief Executive,
> Campbell Soup Co., as quoted by Meredith
> Chen in the *Los Angeles Times*, 3/19/89

The barriers to women in the business world are breaking down and
will continue to do so in the nineties. In many male-dominated companies and industries, where EEOC requirements have forced more
responsibilities for women and minorities, women have done splen-
didly. Thus, the stigma attached to being female has begun to
lessen—and even disappear—in some industries.

Where The Welcome Mat Is Out

Industries in which we see women genuinely welcome are: education, retailing, travel, fashion, design/architecture, packaged goods
(particularly hair care and cosmetics), publishing, advertising/PR, lei-
sure/entertainment, law—there are many women judges today—
real estate, and government.

Corporate functions in which we see the welcome signs growing
are human resources, advertising/PR and sales/marketing.

"**Two-thirds** of the new entrants to the labor force in the 1990s
will be women—making child care, parental and family leave,
and flexible work places all issues."
- Ann McLaughlin, former U.S. Secretary of Labor, discussing
  statistics from "Project 2000" by the Bureau Labor Statistics
  and "Workforce 2000," a study commissioned by the Labor
  Department, as quoted in the *Los Angeles Times,* 4/2/89

Significant Headway Is Being Made

Industries in which women are making good strides are finance and
banking, consulting/counseling services, medicine/health care, office
products, high technology, and sporting goods.

Corporate functions in which we are seeing progress are finance/
accounting, office management/administration, and purchasing (except in industrial goods).

"**Women who are not allowed** by the corporation to get back
on track [after parenting] will be apt to leave and go elsewhere
where they are not treated like second-class citizens."
- Jerome M. Rosow, President, Work in America Institute
  research group, as quoted by Meredith Chen in the
  Los Angeles Times, 3/19/89

It's Still Tough Here

Industries that still pose a problem for women are aviation/space,
religious/ministry, automotive/transportation, building/construction,
utilities, energy, industrial products and services, and food processing
and distribution.

Corporate functions in which it is still rough-going are R & D, engineering, production/operation, and labor/industrial relations.

A major advantage for women in business is their tendency to nurture, to be sensitive and intuitive. Men tend to be less so. This all stems from our American upbringing and probably won't change for several decades to come, if even then. Boys are taught to be ambitious, decisive, analytical, and unemotional. Girls are taught to be more imaginative, creative, and caring for the emotional side of things.

All of this can mean that women are extremely capable at interpersonal efforts such as group development, team building, and conflict resolution. We believe that these activities in particular will provide women with very rapid advancement in the nineties.

Any special advice for female/minority/older candidates?

"Present yourself as needed by the company, and there should be no reason you'd not be a serious candidate."
> • Barbara Mitchell, Director of Human Resources, Host International

---

"Play it as if they are not a minority. Applicants who point out their minority status sometimes distract from their qualifications."
> • Doug Cooper, Vice President/Personnel, Valero Energy Corporation

---

"Look for an advantage and use it."
> • Michael Sweet, Director, Compensation, Benefits and Human Resources Systems, Paramount Pictures Corporation

---

Strategies for the 90s

Trust The System?

Do, and you'll lose! Despite protestations to the contrary—in speeches, in recruiting material, in annual reports, wherever—the goal of the corporate system in the nineties (or anytime, for that matter) is not to develop you and your career potential. Rather, the system has been set up to get the maximum work out of you. Your development is *your* problem. You'd better understand that fact and act accordingly. To do otherwise is pure naivete.

How can a candidate best use a human resource department?

"**H.R. people are like anyone else:** they need to be stroked. Through this process, the candidate can learn much about the inner workings of a company and become better able to make a career decision."

> • Russ Ringl, Corporate Director, Human Resources, American Medical Transport, Inc.

"**Either know someone** in the human resource department or avoid it altogether. During the lean times, employment functions have become more effective in screening out."

> • Doug Cooper, Vice President/Personnel, Valero Energy Corporation

How thorough a knowledge of your company do you expect a candidate to have when he or she arrives for an interview?

"**Some homework must be done.** And don't misspell the company's name, the chairman's name, or my name."

> • M. Jennings, Senior Vice President/Personnel, Gannett Company

CHAPTER SEVEN

HOW DO I GET WHAT I WANT?

Webster defines "negotiation" as "a conferring, discussing, or bargaining to reach an agreement." To reach an agreement is, of course, the goal of *all* negotiation. However, when it comes to employment, we might add four important words: "satisfactory to *both* parties!"

If you have accepted a compensation package that is substantially less than you had hoped for or feel you deserve, it is unlikely that you will perform up to your potential in the job. If the employer, for whatever reason, gives in to demands that are substantially greater than the upper limits established for the position, you can be certain that, unless you perform spectacularly, he or she will be unhappy with just about everything you do. Of course, more than likely, if your demands are out of line, the decision-maker will simply end the discussion with "thanks, but no thanks" and show you the door—in which case you may have lost a job that might have been right for you.

Negotiating an employment contract or compensation package must ultimately be a "win-win" situation. Both parties must be satisfied and comfortable with the outcome. Otherwise, resentment will tarnish the relationship from the very beginning.

How Do I Decide What To Ask For?

The first step is to determine the job's upper and lower salary limits. In most companies, these limits have been established for every job function as a matter of policy. Whatever bargaining you do should be conducted within these boundaries.

How Can I Determine Salary Limits without Asking?

There are many ways to arrive at a reasonably close estimate, but keep in mind that your major concern is the *upper* limit. You should have already established your own minimum needs. If a job can't meet those, then there is little point in negotiating further. The value in knowing a job's lowest compensation level is that you have a better idea of the spread between the lower and upper limits. In other words, how much room for bargaining exists?

If the position for which you are being interviewed is a natural extension of your career path, you should already have a pretty good idea of the logical salary range. If not, here are some suggestions that will be helpful.

Search the want ads (in newspapers as well as trade journals for your industry) for job descriptions that are close to or match the position for which you are being interviewed. Average the high and low salaries being offered to arrive at a median figure.

If your interview has been arranged by a third party, say an employment agency or search firm, ask them for the information. If they don't have it, request that they get it.

If you have a friend within the company, or in a similar position with another company, question him or her about compensation. Or ask a friend's friend. Use your network!

Do some library research. You will find a number of books that provide salary information for specific functions. This information is generally broken down by geographic location as well. Again, talk with your local librarian.

Once I Have This Salary Information, How Does It Help?

In a number of ways. First, it prevents you from wasting valuable time interviewing for a job that can't satisfy your personal financial needs.

Also, having advance knowledge of these compensation figures provides you the time necessary to strategize your approach to bargaining. If you have a firm idea of what you are trying to achieve in a negotiation, and you are convinced that your goals are reasonable, you will be more confident and assured during the bargaining process. Just as in every aspect of the job search, preparation is the key to success.

You should also consider other factors that can influence the strategy of your compensation goals. Knowing how long a job has been vacant, for instance, can be of great value. If you discover, for example, that the company has had trouble filling the position for which you are interviewing, you might want to begin negotiations nearer to the position's upper salary limit. On the other hand, if the opening has just occurred, and there seems to be no rush to fill it, you may want to scale down your request.

The company's interest in you is something you should also take into consideration. If you perceive it to be only lukewarm, you may want to temper your salary request accordingly. Of course the opposite is also true, in which case you may choose to stretch your request a bit.

Sometimes negotiating a compensation package that places you near or at the upper limit of the job's range can create problems further down the line. Short of a policy change, you will find that raises are hard to come by. You may also find yourself the object of resentment among associates who have been with the company much longer than you, but are being paid less. Either situation can result in conflict that may be counterproductive to your own well-being.

How Else Can I Prepare for Negotiations?

Compare your needs with those of the company. Discover what the company is looking for in a candidate and why. Having determined that information, you will be in a better position to assess your own value. Remember, an employer probably won't want to even begin negotiations unless he or she feels that you can satisfy a company need. With that understanding—and all of the knowledge you have acquired through research—you should find yourself in a pretty strong bargaining position. Furthermore, unless your situation has become desperate, you always can walk away from an unsatisfactory offer.

Remember, though—as we pointed out earlier—that employment negotiations must be approached as "win-win" exercises. Both parties to an agreement must be comfortable with the results, or no one wins in the long run. You must be prepared, just as the employer must be, to make concessions or trade-offs in order to reach a mutually supportive agreement.

What Should I Do if I Am Asked How Much I Was Paid in My Last Job?

Don't answer, unless you are forced to. By indicating your former salary, one of two things can happen, both of them bad! If your former salary was well below the upper limits of the new position, chances are you will be offered much less than you might otherwise have gotten. On the other hand, if your former salary exceeded the new job's upper limit, you may be closed out of an opportunity before negotiations begin.

How do you respond when a candidate sidesteps the issue of former salary?

"I get the applicant to start talking about starting salary and progress to the current job."
> • John L. Hanson, Vice President/Human Resources, Parker Hannifin Corporation

---

How Can I Avoid Revealing that Information?

Simply try to sidestep or to turn the question around when it comes up. Respond with something like this: "May I suggest that perhaps were talking apples and oranges, since the responsibilities and environment here are quite different than those in my former [or present] company. Thus, what I'm now making [or was making] doesn't really apply. What do you have in mind as a range for the job?"

Or try this approach: "Since this position isn't the same as my last [or current] job, I wouldn't want salary to become a deciding factor. What range do you see for the job?"

Or this one: "Once we've become more familiar with each other, I'm sure salary won't be a problem." This tactic may buy you some time. You can then subtly ask questions about the past salary range, about their salary budget, or about what the latest incumbent made. It may also give you more of a chance to sell yourself before you get down to negotiations.

You might also try our all time favorite (generally best for middle or upper-level managers): "Well, at (your current or former company), I enjoyed a generous but complicated financial package. It consisted of salary, health and dental benefits, bonuses, incentives, a pension plan and several different perks. I'm sure that package is quite different than the one you offer here. What do you have in mind for the job?" When they answer, you say, "That's a good place to start talking." The negotiating psychology here is that the interviewer making the offer knows his or her company's financial package is complicated and is therefore sympathetic to *your* complicated package. Since you are not going to work for "only your former salary" (after all, you had all those other elements—maybe even a car and a club membership!), why go into all the details of your package. The purpose for asking what you're making is really only to find out if you are in the company's financial-package ballpark anyway. So, what *you're* saying is, "Tell me what you have in mind as a package."

We call this cat-and-mouse game "ratcheting up." The idea behind it is to create an image of something the company wants, without letting them know what it costs, which will make them want it all the more.

An everyday example of this tactic might be if you and a friend go to a movie on a Saturday evening. On the way, you pass a shoe store, and you see in the window the most fantastic pair of shoes you have seen in a long time. You *must* have those shoes! But the store is closed and there is no price tag on the shoes. Rats! During the movie you think of nothing but those shoes. You pass the store again on the way back to your car. Fabulous shoes, but you can't have them tonight. Double rats!

The next morning, you go back to the shoe store to buy the shoes, but it's Sunday, and the store is closed on Sunday. Triple rats! All day Sunday, it's the shoes, the shoes. Finally, it's Monday at lunch. Forget the corned beef sandwich; you head for the shoe store, right? And viola! It's open. You rush in and ask the price of the shoes. What?! That's all? We'll bet dollars to donuts the quoted price will be signifi-cantly *lower* than you would be willing to pay. Why? Because in your desire to possess those shoes, the price of which you didn't know, you ratcheted up their value in your mind—over three days—way beyond the actual cost.

In the same way, you ratchet-up your value to companies with which you are negotiating. But don't let them know your cost! Ob-viously, if the interviewer is insistent, and you sense a dangerous sit-uation developing, give in and provide the information. What we are saying is that it is definitely to your advantage *not* to reveal this infor-mation, but not to the point of jeopardizing the interview and per-haps the job.

In all fairness, however, we should tell you that the results of our survey of human resources directors and search firms indicated a unanimous displeasure with any candidate who refuses to answer the question. That, of course, is to be expected, as it's their job to get that information.

Nevertheless, we still feel that it's worth a try to avoid revealing former salary, as long as you are sensitive to the interviewer's mood and degree of patience.

How do you respond when a candidate sidesteps the issue of former salary?

"**It depends.** I know I'd do the same on the other side of the fence until an appropriate time, *when* I knew there was an interest."

    • **Beverly Fuentes, Vice President/Staffing and Employment, Bank of America**

"All right, Winslow, I'll play your silly game. Did your last job pay between $250 and $800 a week?"

"I tell them that salary information is easy to get and that I'd rather they tell me. Ninety-nine percent of the time they do, so I don't see this as a problem."

    • Denny Wheeler, Manager, Corporate Human Resources, B. F. Goodrich

So Far, You've Concentrated on Salary. What About Benefits?

A complete compensation package does include additional perks and benefits. Until now, we have discussed the matter of salary exclusively because, in most cases, weekly income is a candidate's primary concern. But in addition to base salary, you should be aware of the many other benefits that may be available, either as standard company policy or through negotiation. Each of the items on the following list should be explored during the negotiation process:

- Bonus
- Salary review
- Profit sharing
- Stock options
- Credit union or thrift plan
- Insurance: medical, dental, vision, life, dependents
- Savings plans (401K)
- Retirement fund
- Company car and gas card
- Parking
- Expense allowance
- Vacations and holidays
- Sick leave
- Association memberships
- Education: reimbursement and in-house programs
- Subsidized relocation

Use these items as bargaining chips. If they can't give you one item, ask for another. Trade one for another. Strategize, and play all of this for everything it's worth, which can be a lot.

How Long Should Negotiations Take?

That depends on the organization with which you are dealing and on the level of employment you are after. Ordinarily, you can expect to have two meetings, but the higher up the position, the longer it will take.

"Mr. Winslow, since you've lowered your salary demand to $70,000, we've decided to raise our offer to $20,000."

Remember, you are negotiating for more than just base salary and benefits. You must also have a clearly defined description of the job: general responsibilities, title, accountabilities, formal company expectations, informal company expectations (which might include socializing with the "right" people or protecting non-producers), and so on. These informal expectations may run you into value-clashes,

so we urge that you carefully evaluate these areas of unwritten expectations before accepting an offer. If you are perceived as being
aloof or unwilling to participate in company social life, it could lead
to your not being accepted by your peers and by "the brass," which
could lead to eventual termination. These are areas that fall into the
political arena. As you know, every organization has its own brand
of politics, so be prepared to deal with it.

Now, a very important piece of advice. The fact that you have en-
tered into negotiations for a job is no reason to halt your job search;
in fact, that is about the worst thing you can do. No matter how
positive you may be, regardless of how serious an offer may appear,
there are about a hundred reasons why an offer can be withdrawn.
*Keep your campaign going at full speed until you have something in writing
or have actually begun your new job.*

Should I Get Something in Writing When an Offer Is Made?

Absolutely. Or, perhaps more properly, you should absolutely try.
You won't always succeed (and it shouldn't be a deal-breaker if you
fail), but if a decision-maker is reluctant to confirm an offer in writing, you should proceed with a degree of skepticism.

When you receive an offer, find out if there are any further conditions preliminary to your employment. These conditions might include a medical examination or further reference checks. Carefully
review the offer with your future boss, and make certain he or she
concurs with your understanding.

Then ask if you may have a written confirmation of the offer. You
may explain that you have other pending offers and that you are reluctant to refuse them without written assurance that you have this
job. Be sure that the memorandum of understanding includes the
fact that you are being offered a specific job—it must be fully described—with a specific title and salary, as well as other negotiated
benefits. Be sure your starting date is clearly identified.

If your future boss refuses to put his or her offer in writing, or cites
company policy as forbidding it, offer to write a letter of acceptance
in duplicate, including all of the above details, and have your new
boss sign and return one copy as confirmation. If he or she can't write

anything because of company policy but you still want to proceed, send your confirmation/acceptance letter by "return receipt requested" mail. That way, you will know the boss received it, in case there is a problem down the line.

What If My Boss Simply Refuses To Put Anything in Writing?

If that's the case, you will just have to base your expectations on trust and on what you have learned about the company through research. As long as you don't stop your job-search campaign because of the offer, the worst that can happen is the disappointment you will feel if a job doesn't actually materialize.

The issue of written confirmation depends to some extent on the level of job you are after. If you happen to be a senior executive, it is likely that you will negotiate an employment contract and perhaps employ the services of an attorney for advice and counsel. On the other hand, if the job is entry-level or low-level, it is unlikely that you will get anything more than a blank stare in return for your request to put the offer in writing. It's for everyone in between that we make this recommendation, and remember, it's only a recommendation. If it works, you have a degree of security that you wouldn't otherwise have. If it doesn't work, don't let yourself get lulled into a certainty that isn't yet a certainty.

Strategies for the 90s

On Getting to the Top in the 90s

"The next century's corporate chief must have multi-environment, multi-country, multi-functional, maybe even multi-company, multi-industry experience."
* Ed Dunn, Corporate Vice President, Whirlpool Corp., as quoted in the *Wall Street Journal*, "Going Global," by Amanda Bennett, 2/27/89

In the decade ahead, as well as beyond, the past career of any member of senior management will have contained three key elements. So, if the top of the heap is your goal, here is what you will need.

Element #1: Cross-Functional Knowledge

Cross-functional knowledge means knowledge about each of the following functions, which are key to the managing of the business:

- Operations/manufacturing
- Sales/marketing
- Finance
- People management

Cross-functional knowledge doesn't mean you must have been an actual manager in each of these areas. It does mean, however, that you must have been closely involved with each of them in some way. In other words, you must be able to show clear accomplishment, as a member of a team, with those functions.

Let's say, for example, that you are an operations manager and are responsible for building a new plant. This project involves not only operations knowledge but lots of financial involvement as well. Or perhaps you are a marketing manager and are introducing a new product requiring lots of modifications of facilities. Although you are in marketing, this project also requires lots of operations expertise as well. The successful completion of either of these projects indicates a good bit of "elbow-rubbing" experience or cross-functional knowledge of another function in the company.

Of course, don't forget where your real strengths are; that's where you'll succeed and star. Don't be conned into a zig-zagging management path, into managing functions requiring other skills than those in which you are strong. For example, if your strengths are in marketing, don't get talked into a finance job. You won't succeed (or if you do, it will be at the cost of your health). "Rub Elbows" with finance on a common project instead.

Element #2: Profit and Loss Experience

In order to gain profit and loss experience, you should try not to be limited to staff jobs. Run a plant or a sales operation.

Element #3: Visibility

You must make sure that people know who you are. Your boss and your boss's boss have to know of your accomplishments. An occasional memo to both your boss and *his or her* boss about a particularly stunning performance of yours—describe only results for *the company!*—can't hurt. But only do it occasionally, and only when your achievements warrant such a memo.

Also get on the speaking circuit. Write and deliver several speeches about your specialty and its relationship to current events. Don't give self-serving "here's what I do" speeches, but ones that have political, social, or economic significance regarding your specialty. If you are an international marketing manager, for instance, you could talk about the impact of foreign competition. A human resources manager could talk about downsizing techniques. A finance manager could discuss investment strategies for greater cash flow. There are all kinds of local business, social, and fraternal associations that have weekly or monthly meetings, and they are always looking for speakers. Then there is the local Chamber of Commerce; of course, a speech there provides terrific visibility. Then don't forget to let your boss and his or her boss know about your speaking engagements.

Next, write articles for local and/or industry periodicals. Most local newspapers also print viewpoint contributions, as do business journals and industry publications. Submit a few articles. They just may get published, and then watch the corporate eyes focus on you.

Incidentally, giving speeches and writing articles are good ways to make yourself visible to the head-hunter community too.

And be innovative. Create projects, methodologies, or plans, for example, that require approval from two or three levels up the line: your boss's boss and his or her boss.

Element #4: A Mentor

Find a friend in upper management, someone who likes you and likes your style. His or her advice and counsel, as well as "good words for you at the right time," can create a real breakthrough.

To be competitive in the coming decade, a young man or woman will need:

"numeric/computer capability (mathematics), understanding of economics, and psychology training relative to group management, team-building, etc., [young people will] not necessarily [need] management skills."
  • Vera Blanchet, Vice President/Human Resources, Corporate Headquarters, California Savings & Loan Association

---

Strategies for the 90s

Where Do You Stand?

Every six months, anyone in an executive or administrative position should assess where he or she stands. Even if you received a glowing performance review seven or eight months ago, things change. A new boss comes in who has different standards than your former boss; your division or the company performs poorly; or the company is facing the threat or actuality of a takeover.

So, is the handwriting on the wall for you? Is the ax over your head? If you don't know, here is a simple quiz you can take that will give you a pretty good idea of where you stand with your present employer. In fact, it is a good idea to repeat this quiz every six months.

  1. Are you regularly asked to participate in highly important projects of your group or division?

"I've been asked to test your computer literacy, Mr. Winslow."

2. Are your ideas and suggestions well received by your superiors?
3. Are you among the first to hear about important decisions, changes, and projects?
4. Have you been included in the administrative planning and/or budgeting processes recently?
5. Are you getting frequent increases in salary and/or other compensation?
6. Do your superiors openly express good opinions of you?
7. Do your superiors react favorably to your friendly overtures?
8. Do your peers respond positively to your requests for action?

9. Do your peers applaud (rather than resent) your
   accomplishments?
10. Does your boss support you and call others' attention to your
    skills and accomplishments?
11. Have you been given more responsibility recently?
12. Is your boss comfortable with you as a subordinate (as
    opposed to being threatened by you)?
13. Does your boss credit you publicly for your accomplishments
    (as opposed to taking credit him or herself)?
14. Does the frequency of your promotions compare favorably
    with that of your peers?
15. Do you have a mentor in the company, a higher-ranking
    person who voluntarily serves as your coach and supporter?
16. Is your company supportive in personal matters, such as
    illness, family problems, and child care?
17. Is your title one that indicates you are on the fast track
    within the company?
18. Does your office compare favorably with those of your peers
    in its location and appointments (carpeting, furniture, art)?

Give yourself one point for every "yes" answer. If you score fifteen
or better, you are probably secure in your job. If you wind up with
less than fifteen but more than ten points, you'd better watch your
p's and q's. If you have ten or fewer points, chances are the skids are
being greased for your departure, and you'd better leave while it is
still your own idea.

CHAPTER EIGHT

FUTURE WINNERS—
THE WINNING JOBS OF THE NINETIES

"**There's no doubt** in our minds that [the aging population] is going to be a major area of focus, both at the retail level and the supplier level. I think you're going to see changes in the way we design our stores, the way we do business, the way we package our products."

> • Stuart Rosenthal, Executive Vice President,
> Von's Supermarkets, as quoted in the
> *Los Angeles Herald Examiner*, 4/24/89

As we have suggested throughout this book, change is as inevitable as death and taxes. While some changes occur suddenly, usually the result of an unexpected technological breakthrough, others—the majority, in fact—are predictable to some degree. For the most part, changes are the logical result of a *series* of developments. For example, one did not have to be a seer to anticipate the erosion of the market for manual typewriters once the electric typewriter had been introduced. Nor did it require any special genius to anticipate a lessening demand for the electric typewriter once the personal computer and the word processor had become widely available.

We have already identified a variety of market forces that are clearly visible today. These forces—our aging population, the globalization of business, and advanced technology, to name a few—are, in fact, the harbingers of change. While the full extent of this change may be impossible to predict accurately in advance, it is possible to draw some broad, general conclusions with regard to growth industries and future career paths.

In this chapter, we will discuss some occupational fields that should grow and prosper in the decades ahead.

High Tech

From lasers to medical technology to superconductivity and continued computer evolution, the high tech industry will only continue to grow and change ever more rapidly. Our daily lives will become more and more dependent on these advances, creating jobs in research, development, production, marketing, and administration in the high-tech industry, as well as creating jobs that involve teaching laypeople how to understand, use, and apply the new technologies.

"It will be very difficult for an individual skilled in only a single discipline to reach the top."
- Douglas Danford, former Chairman,
  Westinghouse Electric Co.,
  as quoted in the *Wall Street Journal*, "Going Global,"
  by Amanda Bennett, 2/27/89

Space Exploration

Regardless of government budget problems, space will continue to be a growth industry. Undoubtedly, commercial possibilities for satellites and other vehicles, even space stations, will cause private enterprise to join with the government in further exploration and development. We will also see more of a global effort here, with many other countries entering the space arena. There should be all kinds of opportunities in space: space welders, miners, mechanics, planetary engineers, and space botanists, in addition to the tens of thousands of office administrative positions necessary to support the entire effort.

Leisure and Travel

With an older population that has considerable spending power, we will see an increased demand for country clubs, recreational vehicles, cruises, air travel, senior centers and the many activities conducted there, senior bowling leagues, senior golf and tennis clubs, adult theme parks (such as Epcot center and the Smithsonian Air and Space Museum), and shopping center "mall-walking." Two-worker households will also be able to take more expensive vacations, likely involving more air travel (less car travel) and more hotel lodging (instead of staying with friends or relatives). Entertainment of all kinds—theaters, movies, theme parks, concerts, and so on—will benefit from the rather well-heeled retirees, as well as the two-income baby boomers.

"We are experiencing the turbulent process of a restructuring of the global economy. The United States will certainly remain one of the leading international economic powers for the foreseeable future, but it will never again account for nearly one-half of total global industrial production."
  • David M. Gordon, Professor of Economics, New School for Social Research, as quoted in the *Los Angeles Times,* 5/21/89

Housing

The changing demographic make-up of U.S. households, as well as the coming senior boom, will cause tremendous change in the housing needs of Americans. With more single people living alone or in non-traditional couples and with fewer children in those households, smaller homes will be in demand. With the senior boomers reaching early retirement at the end of the decade, there will be increased need for safe, controlled retirement communities. Enormous opportunities exist in this area in preparation for the third millennium. The design, building, and staffing of these retirement complexes will employ many hundred of thousands.

Ocean Exploration

It is predicted that the next "world farm" will be the oceans, that the oceans will soon feed much of the world's population. Thus, we will see the need for "ocean farmers," workers trained in the agribusiness of raising aquatic foods. We will also see opportunities for ocean-miners, technicians, and undersea support services personnel, such as hotel managers and service employees.

Health Care

With America aging, there will be increased demand for health services, particularly toward the end of the decade as the baby-boomers begin to retire. Daniel Calahan, Ph.D., in his 1987 book *Setting Limits* says we must begin to think about health in terms of improving the quality of life for our elderly, such as providing long-term care and home care. This trend will provide new opportunities for nursing and other in-home services. Particularly for the terminally ill, long-term care and aid will also be provided by hospices, a level of health-care service that is growing rapidly and that requires medical services as well as support services.[1]

Food and Beverage

We are in for big opportunities in the food and beverage industry due to changes in our households and to the graying of America. Experts predict that the convenience foods industry will show extraordinary growth and opportunity in the nineties, primarily because more single people, childless couples, and older people will demand these foods since they are easier and faster to prepare.

Insurance

The older Americans become, the more insurance they will want (life insurance in particular). The senior boom will create much opportunity for this industry.

Education and Training

With industries and jobs disappearing and new ones developing at breakneck speed, re-education and re-training are going to be in great demand. Teachers and trainers with specific in-depth knowledge of job skills that are in high demand will be kept very busy.

Radio and Television

Experts predict that radio and cable TV will become more like special-interest magazines, concentrating on clearly defined viewer interests. This phenomenon is sometimes called "narrowcasting" and is seen in such special formats as at-home shopping, or programming that is all news, all finance, all travel, all fashion, all weather, all health, and so on. These programs will continue to grow in number and will become more specific in their audience focus, creating new opportunities for the entire spectrum of radio and TV production.

Other Winners

Experts such as the World Future Society feel that other job categories will emerge and grow in the nineties, such as toxic waste disposal, bionic medical technicians,[2] hibernation specialists, volcanologists, shyness and wellness consultants, and leisure counselors. William Johnston of the Hudson Institute sees bright prospects in food service, hotel management, engineering, basic science, business services, financial services, human resources, teaching, and maintenance and repair.[3]

Among hot occupations for the nineties, the U.S. government's Occupational Outlook Handbook lists medical records technicians, computer programmers and system analysts, dental hygienists, accountants, lawyers, paralegals, and employment interviewers. The

tight labor market will also cause other things to happen. Mitchell
Fromstein, president of Manpower, Inc., a personnel firm, says there
will be a shift away from forced early retirement, extending the work
life of reliable employees during the nineties.[4] Others predict a large
increase in the use of temporary and part-time help to fill in gaps in
the work force. This trend will provide opportunities for retirees who
want to work part-time, as well as for women with children who
want some extra income.

Notes

1. Dychtwald, Ken, and Joe Flower, *Age Wave* (Los Angeles: Tarcher, 1989),
pp. 79–81.
2. "Careers Beyond the Millenium," *Personal Report* (New York: February
1989).
3. "Jobs of Tomorrow," *Personal Report* (New York: March 1989).
4. James Flanigan, "Labor Shortage is Opportunity in the Making," *Los Angeles Times* (April 30, 1989).

APPENDIX—SAMPLE RESUMES

SKILL-BASED RESUME SAMPLE

(Name)
(Address and Telephone Numbers)

A goals-oriented, senior-level executive with nine years of full profit and loss responsibility. A broadly based manager with 22 years of finance and manufacturing experience in the metal-working and electronics industries.

- Planned and implemented the turnaround of a Fortune 100 company's $27 million division.
- Developed financial controls and systems that allowed more accurate costing, pricing, and increased profits.
- Restructured manufacturing capabilities and capacity to satisfy a 400 percent sales increase.
- Directed the development of an MRP II system, as well as other management information systems.

An articulate systematic manager who builds organizations through analysis, motivation, and communication.

SIGNIFICANT ACCOMPLISHMENTS

General Management
- Developed and implemented short- and long-range plans and strategies, which in four years increased annual sales from $5 million to $27 million and employees from 85 to 250.
- Turned around a company in four years from a pre-tax loss, to a 27 percent pre-tax profit.
- Directed four labor union negotiations, resulting in below-cost-of-living increases, employees' cost-sharing of benefits package, and switching of pension from Teamsters to in-house plan.

Finance
- Designed job cost systems that identified non-profitable products.
- Developed departmental costing that allowed reduced operating costs and more accurate product pricing.

Manufacturing
- Increased factory self-sufficiency from 52 percent to 93 percent by purchasing and upgrading equipment; enlarged plant by 52 percent.
- Implemented a fully computerized MRP II system that improved customer deliveries by 36 percent and reduced manufacturing costs by 16 percent.

- Introduced a "group technology" system for part design, integrated routing, and estimating.

- Upgraded data processing capability from a manual card system to current computer technology.

EXPERIENCE

LUKUS CORPORATION   1971–Present
Lakeview, New Jersey

President, Fastening Systems   1976–1985
- Products include aircraft fasteners and specialty hydraulic components.
- Responsible for full profit and loss, as well as reorganization of this $27 million division.

Vice President, Administration/Controller   1973–1976
- Directed and supervised all financial operations, human resources, and data processing.

Controller   1971–1973
- Reorganized all accounting functions and introduced data processing.

DEMUS CORPORATION   1969–1971
Pasadena, California

Corporate Controller, Division Controller

LESTIC CORPORATION   1965–1969
Pasadena, California

Manager, Corporate Accounting; Manager, General Ledger; Financial Analyst

SIMUS CORPORATION   1960–1965
Detroit, Michigan

Senior Financial Analyst; Manager, Material and Labor Audit; Cost Accountant

EDUCATION

Michigan State University, B.S. in Business

SKILL-BASED RESUME SAMPLE

(Name)
(Address and Telephone Numbers)

Fifteen years of experience encompassing all aspects of corporate EDP functions. A results-oriented executive whose experience includes:

- Responsible for information systems of a $5 billion health insurance company.
- Developed systems to meet long-range plans.
- Managed professional groups of up to 250 people.
- Reduced employee turnover from 40 percent to 10 percent, while increasing productivity 180 percent.

A creative and action-oriented manager who uses a humanistic approach to manage change and maximize productivity.

SIGNIFICANT ACCOMPLISHMENTS

Systems Development
- Created a highly productive work force and climate using improved project and people management techniques.
- Developed many new systems using advanced technologies and innovation in the areas of management information, marketing, finance, operations, large customer accounts, hospitals, and the medical community.
- Established several new functions including information center, development center, EDP training, EDP standards and procedures, data base administration, hardware/software planning, system performance administration, and documentation center.

Corporate Management
- Determined long-range plans and policies for senior executive steering committee.
- Directed corporate-wide projects that significantly impacted other divisions within the company, such as HMO operations.

Data Processing
- Responsible for a staff of over 200 people at a large IBM data center, which achieved a high performance level for several IMS on-line applications.
- Managed a data communication network of 1300 terminals throughout 11 western states.

- Upgraded the data center with new mainframe computers, including acquisition of new equipment and sale of outdated equipment.

EXPERIENCE

MAXI-HEALTH   1980–Present
San Jose, California

Director, Systems Development
- Responsible for meeting corporate data-processing and informational needs.

HEALTH CARE PLUS   1979–1980
Seattle, Washington

Manager, Data Processing Services
- Accountable for corporate data center and technical support functions.

Manager, Application Development and Support Services   1976–1979
- Responsible for corporate systems, data base administration, hardware/software planning, systems performance administration, EDP standards and procedures, and EDP training.

Various managerial, supervisory, and systems   1970–1976
developmental positions

EDUCATION

University of California at Los Angeles, Graduate School
of Business Administration   April 1981
Effective Management Program Certificate

University of Illinois, School of Public Health   June 1980
National Health Care Institute

SKILL-BASED RESUME SAMPLE

(Name)
(Address and Telephone Numbers)

A marketing/public relations specialist with over six years diversified experience in consumer products marketing, law, journalism, and natural resources investments. A competitive, enthusiastic, well-organized achiever who sets and achieves goals, with excellent verbal and written communication skills, as well as skills in innovative problem-solving techniques.

SIGNIFICANT ACCOMPLISHMENTS

- Improved projected sales potential at a critical transition time for a major consumer products company by arranging a special national sales meeting.
- Wrote collateral and packaging copy that supported the successful repositioning of a $65-million hair care line.
- Developed an evaluation procedure for formula-tested new product lines.
- Recruited and interviewed professional-level and support-staff candidates for a law firm and developed an orientation program for new employees.

PROFESSIONAL EXPERIENCE

HAIR CARE, INC.   1985–Present
Los Angeles, California

Marketing Assistant
- Assisted in repositioning an entire hair care line.
- Evaluated creative and consumer promotion data in order to formulate a realistic marketing plan.

SAMSON & JONES (law firm)   1984–1985
Los Angeles, California

Administrative Assistant
- Responsible for office management and organization.
- Assisted in organizing key functions of firm.
- Organized and maintained all employee records.

HEMPHILL & WOOD (lawyers)   1983
Beverly Hills, California

Administrative Assistant
- Supervised all general office duties and oversaw secretarial work flow.

THE TEXAS STAR   1982–1983
Dallas, Texas

Assistant Sports Editor
- Covered major state and national sporting events, including play-by-play, personality profiles, and game previews.

DALLAS FLIGHT   1981–1982
Love Field, Dallas, Texas

Flight Operator

BEST ENERGY CORPORATION   1979–1981
Fort Worth, Texas

Assistant Office Manager
- Responsible for personnel records, recruitment of office staff, and general administrative duties.

EDUCATION

University of Texas, Journalism
B.A. DEGREE

AFFILIATIONS

Women in Journalism

SKILL-BASED RESUME SAMPLE

(Name)
(Address and Telephone Numbers)

A broad-based tax and financial planning executive with 19 years of progressively responsible experience. Industry experience includes manufacturing, high technology, consumer goods, service companies, and a partnership in a major accounting firm.

- Restructured closely held franchise operations by creating subsidiary to sell franchises on a national basis.
- Generated $2 million savings by creating onshore, captive insurance company.
- Created several *D.I.S.C.s*, generating tax savings of $50,000 to $1 million.

A technically oriented professional whose requirement for quality has generated profits for clients and developed the talents and expertise of subordinates and peers. A strong administrator whose quiet sense of humor enhances his effectiveness on all levels of an organization.

SIGNIFICANT ACCOMPLISHMENTS

Operations
- Restructured large, closely held corporate franchising operations by creating subsidiary to sell franchises on a national basis, creating more than $5 million in franchise fees without incurring additional tax to client.
- Created tax savings of $500,000 for corporation by restructuring terms of bonus arrangements with employees.
- Generated cash flow from tax savings of approximately $2 million by creating onshore captive insurance subsidiary for large multinational corporation.
- Reduced purchase price of a division by $400,000 by creating a leasing subsidiary prior to the purchase, avoiding sales tax on the transfer of the division's equipment.

Mergers, Acquisitions, & Divestitures
- Negotiated approximately $5 million of unique acquisition financing, resulting in favorable sale of client's company.
- Negotiated an increased price on a divestiture by helping buyer company to better understand the tax benefits of the transaction.

- Reduced the purchase price of an acquisition by $1 million through the complex creation of a new subsidiary and conversion of inventory to LIFO method.

Tax Planning
- Developed employment agreement for advertising company, resulting in retention of several talented executives.

Management & Systems
- Created and implemented system for tax department that significantly reduced staff time spent on the billing process, as well as substantially increasing client fees.
- Created and implemented system of monitoring the firm's accounts receivable, which reduced collection time for receivables and consequently reduced interest cost.
- Participated in the creation of a system for monitoring and scheduling the productivity of all tax department professionals.

EXPERIENCE

PRICE & ERNST   1964–Present
St. Louis, Missouri

Tax Partner   1974–Present
- Handle tax planning and tax compliance needs of approximately 150 corporate, partnership, individual, estate, and trust clients, including financial statement implications for corporate clients.

Tax Department
- Prepare tax returns, review of tax returns, tax research, accrual reviews, and supervision of tax staff.

Audit Staff
- Reconcile bank accounts, audit balance sheet accounts, and responsible for planning and completing audit.

EDUCATION

Certified Public Accountant; Certified in New York, California, and Louisiana
Columbia University, New York, New York; Graduate Tax Work, 1967
Miami University, Miami, Florida; B.S., Magna Cum Laude
   Outstanding Achievement Award for Scholarship and Athletic Excellence
   Philosophy Award
Yale University, New Haven, Connecticut

AFFILIATIONS

American Institute of Certified Public Accountants
California Society of Certified Public Accountants
Chairman of Task Force Investigating Freedom of Information Act,
Committee on Taxation
San Diego Chamber of Commerce, Federal Affairs Committee
Life Insurance and Trust Council of San Diego

CHRONOLOGICAL RESUME SAMPLE

(Name)
(Address and Telephone Numbers)

Extensive management experience within the entertainment industry. Particular expertise in operations, marketing, and sales. Achieved significant success in start-up and turnaround situations.

PROFESSIONAL EXPERIENCE

LONE STAR PICTURES   1986–Present
Hollywood, California
  Chief Operating Officer
  General responsibilities of this position include establishing a national distribution system to market programming to television stations. Specific duties include: developing business plans, defining market needs, preparing operating budgets and sales objectives, packaging and marketing product, establishing sales territories, designing rate structures, staffing the sales force, and conducting contract negotiations.

SIGNIFICANT ACCOMPLISHMENTS

- Created and implemented an entirely new business approach to identifying new products and to developing innovative marketing strategies and distribution systems.
- Totally restructured sales systems, achieving $2 million in sales in the first six months.

MEGA-HIT PICTURES   1983–1986
Burbank, California

  Director of Special Marketing, Television Syndication
  General responsibilities included developing, implementing and controlling marketing and sales efforts throughout the United States, as well as directing negotiations and licensing of television programs to stations, including structuring "buy-back" contracts.

SIGNIFICANT ACCOMPLISHMENTS

- Planned and implemented a national marketing and sales effort for the *Selwyn Family* series, which resulted in the surpassing of all sales records for a television series.
- Served as liaison between litigants, averting a multi-million-dollar lawsuit.

ALL-WORLD TELEVISION   1978–1983
Atlanta, Georgia

Sales Executive, Television Syndication

General responsibilities included marketing television programs to local stations, as well as conducting a full range of contract negotiations. During this five-year period, sales volume in the territory increased by 80 percent.

EDUCATION

Colgate University, B.A. in Communications
University of London, England, Graduate Studies in
International Television

CHRONOLOGICAL RESUME

(Name)
(Address and Telephone Numbers)

Nineteen years of Far East business operations, involving the purchasing of consumer and industrial products for U.S. and Canadian markets. Specific skills in licensing, letters of credit, and import/export systems for Far East financial business operations.

PROFESSIONAL EXPERIENCE

LEDACO, INC.   1973–Present
Los Angeles, California

Vice President, Far East Operations

General responsibilities include: sourcing manufacturers and trading companies throughout the Far East, including Korea, Taiwan, Japan, and Hong Kong; establishing banking relations with major banks; sourcing and contracting business relationships with agents, and managing shipping and import activities.

SIGNIFICANT ACCOMPLISHMENTS

- Sourced 25 key trading companies, which resulted in successfully importing over $9 million per year.
- Initiated a start-up procurement program in Korea, which led to capturing an exclusive Canadian market for $14 million in new business.
- Set up import/export department that decreased distribution delays by 45 percent in first year.

CAMEO, INC.   1969–1973
Los Angeles, California

Manager, Far East Procurement

General responsibilities included establishing an international trading operation for the Far East. Duties included locating and training offshore agents to buy and inspect consumer products; initiating banking relations; and establishing shipping schedules, pricing and manufacturing costs.

SIGNIFICANT ACCOMPLISHMENTS

- Contracted with 37 manufacturers located in six Far East countries, resulting in successful importing of goods worth over $28 million.
- Successfully set up four major Canadian and European distributors for $9 million of Taiwanese products, surpassing sales goals by 30 percent.
- Developed a unique distribution system to move over $7 million in products, reducing delivery time during peak shipping periods.

EDUCATION

American Institute for Foreign Trade, M.B.A.,
University of Southern California, B.S. in Business Development

CHRONOLOGICAL RESUME SAMPLE

(Name)
(Address and Telephone Numbers)

SUMMARY

Over five years of experience in serving property/casualty policy holders of a major national insurance company. The regional office environment has provided an opportunity to learn and assist policy holders in such areas as claims, policy change, underwriting rules/requirements, coverage interpretation, and overall customer relations.

EXPERIENCE
COASTAL INSURANCE COMPANY, INC.
Wilmington, Delaware

Service Assistant   1979–Present

Junior Service Assistant   1976–1979

- Provided service to policy holders, by telephone and in person, on varied subjects in a high-volume operation. Assisted up to 100 policyholders a day during peak periods.
- Selected by manager to train newly-hired employees in claim processing and policy change functions.
- Suggested revisions for a series of policy-change forms that were tested in the regional office and subsequently adopted by the home office for use in all regions.
- Contributed as a member of the regional office's task force to improve the efficiency of the central filing system.
- Received three company awards for meritorious service to policy holders.

EDUCATION

North High School, Wilmington, Delaware
Graduated 1976, Commercial Course

CHRONOLOGICAL RESUME SAMPLE

(Name)
(Address and Telephone Numbers)

EXPERIENCE

AMERICAN TRANSPORTATION CORPORATION   1979–Present
Pittsburgh, Pennsylvania

Secretary to Corporate Accounting Manager

Responsibilities and skills include all secretarial duties with a specific focus on financial statistical typing, Vydec information processing, and CRT terminal operations.

- Coordinated monthly time allocation reports of 30 department heads for timely preparation of monthly financial management reports.
- Controlled data entry processing and verified over 200 monthly journal entries via CRT, resulting in timely production of general ledger.
- Produced a 44-page monthly confidential management reporting package, consisting of consolidated financial statements and 20 separate detailed analyses; met three to five-day deadline consistently.

TRANS-INTERNATIONAL COMPANY   1977–1979
Pittsburgh, Pennsylvania

Dictaphone Typist to Insurance Manager and underwriters.

Responsible for and skilled in transcribing letters from a dictaphone, as well as typing insurance policies.

DANBURY HIGH SCHOOL   1974–1977
Danbury, Pennsylvania

Participated in Work Study Program, working in school's administrative office after class and during summer vacations.

EDUCATION

Danbury Senior High School, Danbury, Pennsylvania
Graduated with honors. Participated in Business Courses including Business Math, Accounting, Typing, and Office Practice. Received award for Business Person of the Month.

SKILL-BASED RESUME WORKSHEET

(Name) _____

(Address) _____

(City, State, Zip Code) _____

(Telephone Number) _____

BACKGROUND SUMMARY (Your professional footprint, *summarizing* in a few sentences, the industrial and functional areas in which you have worked).

_____

_____

MAJOR ACCOMPLISHMENTS

(Function) _____

- _____
- _____
- _____
- _____
- _____
- _____
- _____
- _____
- _____
- _____

WORK EXPERIENCE

Company _____

Location (City, State) _____

Dates Employed _____

Job Title: _____ Dates: _____

Company _____

Location (City, State) _____

Dates Employed _____

Job Title: _____ Dates: _____

EDUCATION

School _____

Location (City, State) _____

Degree Awarded and Major Field _____

Certificates _____

PROFESSIONAL ASSOCIATIONS (Optional)

PUBLICATIONS (Optional)

CHRONOLOGICAL RESUME WORKSHEET

(Name) _____

(Address) _____

(City, State, Zip Code) _____

(Telephone Number) _____

BACKGROUND SUMMARY (Your professional footprint, *summarizing* in a few sentences, the industrial and functional areas in which you have worked).

_____

_____

_____

_____

_____

_____

WORK EXPERIENCE

Company _____

Location (City, State) _____

Dates Employed _____

  Job Title: _____ Dates: _____

  Scope of Responsibilities: _____

_____

  Accomplishments:

  • _____

  • _____

  • _____

Company _____

Location (City, State) _____

Dates Employed _____

  Job Title: _____ Dates: _____

  Scope of Responsibilities: _____

_____

Accomplishments:
- _____
- _____
- _____

EDUCATION

School _____
Location (City, State) _____
Degree Awarded and Major Field _____
Certificates _____

PROFESSIONAL ASSOCIATIONS (Optional)

PUBLICATIONS (Optional)

BIBLIOGRAPHY
BOOKS

Beatty, Richard H. *The Five Minute Interview.* John Wiley & Sons.
————. *The Complete Job Search Book.* New York: John Wiley & Sons, 1986.
Bolles, Richard Nelsen. *What Color Is Your Parachute?* Berkeley, Ca.: Ten Speed Press, 1972.
Cetron, Marvin J. and Owen Davies. *The Great Job Shakeout of The 1990s.* New York: Simon & Schuster, 1988.
Dawson, Kenneth M. and Sheryl N. Dawson. *Job Search: The Total System.* New York: John Wiley & Sons, 1988.
Dychtwald, Ken, Ph.D. and Joe Flower. *Age Wave.* Los Angeles: Tarcher, 1989.
    Callahan, Daniel, Ph.D. *Setting Limits.* As quoted by Dychtwald and Flower in *Age Wave.* Los Angeles: Tarcher, 1989.
    Bouvier, Leon F. "America's Baby Boom Generation: The Fateful Bulge," *Population Bulletin,* 35, no. 1 (April 1980). As quoted by Dychtwald and Flower.
Falvey, Jack. *What's Next? Career Strategies after 35.* Charlotte, Vt.: Williamson Publishing, 1987.
Hallett, Jeffrey J. *Workplace Visions.* Alexandria, Va.: American Society for Personnel Administration.
Korn, Lester. *The Success Profile.* New York: Simon & Schuster, 1988.
Medley, H. Anthony. *Sweaty Palms: The Neglected Art of Being Interviewed.* Belmont, Ca.: Lifetime Learning Publications, 1978.
Naisbitt, John. *Megatrends.* New York: Warner Books, 1982.
Pell, Arthur R., Ph.D. *How to Sell Yourself On an Interview.* New York: Monarch Press, 1982.

NEWSPAPER ARTICLES

Los Angeles Herald-Examiner
Bernstein, Sharon. "New Market Predictions for an Aging Population." 24 April 1989.
Los Angeles Times
Flanigan, James. "Work Force on its Own as the Rules Shift." 5 March 1989.
Crudele, John. "Looking Ahead to Losers, Winners for Next Century." 19 March 1989.
Chen, Meredith. *Women at Work: A New Debate Is Born.* 19 March 1989.
Pritkin, John. As quoted in "Looking Ahead to Losers, Winners for Next Century." 19 March 1989.
McLaughlin, Ann. "The Pig in the American Python." 2 April 1989.
Peterson, Jonathan. "Rules for Trade With Europe Will Change in 1992. The Atlantic Rim." 30 April 1989.
Flanigan, James. "Labor Shortage Is Opportunity in the Making." 30 April 1989.
Marshall, Tyler. "Europe Busy Closing Doors to Foreigners." 7 May 1989.
Weidenbaum, Murray. "Global Economy and Government." 7 May 1989.
Gordon, David M. "Prepare for Regional Trading Blocks." 21 May 1989.
Sanchez, Jesus. "Rougher Road for RVs." 29 May 1989.
Wall Street Journal
Bennett, Amanda. "Going Global." 27 February 1989.
Hymowitz, Carol. "Day in the Life of Tomorrow's Manager." 20 March 1989.
Malabre, Alfred L., Jr., and Lindley A. Clark, Jr. "Changes in Economy Cause Much Confusion Among Economists." 27 March 1989.

MAGAZINE ARTICLES

Finney, Martha I. "Planning Today for the Future's Changing Shape." *Personnel Administrator* (January 1989): Pages 44–45.

Fisher, Anne B. "The Ever Bigger Boom in Consulting." *Fortune* (April 1989): 113–134.

Personal Report. Jobs of Tomorrow. National Institute of Business Management (March 1989).

———. *MIT Study Notes Changing Role for Middle Managers.* (December 1988).

———. *The Coming BIMODAL Economy.* (February 1989).

———. *Careers Beyond the Millenium.* (February 1989).

"Products on the Rise and on the Wane." *Supermarket Business Magazine.* As quoted in the *Los Angeles Herald Examiner* (24 April 1989).

Zey, Michael G. "When is a Good Time to Leave Your Company?" *National Business Employment Weekly* (August 1986).

PUBLICATIONS

Directory of Executive Recruiters. 1989. Fitzwilliam, N.H.: Kennedy & Kennedy Publishers.

Executive Strategies. 1987. *Goal Setting for the Year 2000.* New York: Institute of Business Management.

———. *Recareering in the 1990s.* 1989. New York: Institute of Business Management.

U.S. Department of Labor, Bureau of Labor Statistics. *Project 2000.* Washington, D.C.: U.S. Government printing Office.

U.S. Department of Labor. *Workforce 2000.* Washington, D.C.: U.S. Government Printing Office.

PUBLICATIONS

INDEX